# The Advanced Deer Hunter's Bible

# The Advanced Deer Hunter's Bible

## John Weiss

*Drawings by John F. Eggert*

BROADWAY BOOKS
NEW YORK

**BROADWAY**

A previous edition of this book was originally published in 1993 by Doubleday, a division of Random House, Inc. It is here reprinted by arrangement with Doubleday.

Broadway Books titles may be purchased for business or promotional use or for special sales. For information, please write to: Special Markets Department, Random House, Inc., 1540 Broadway, New York, NY 10036.

PRINTED IN THE UNITED STATES OF AMERICA

BROADWAY BOOKS and its logo, a letter B bisected on the diagonal, are trademarks of Broadway Books, a division of Random House, Inc.

Visit our website at www.broadwaybooks.com

First Broadway Books trade paperback edition published 2001.

The Library of Congress Cataloging-in-Publication Data has cataloged the previous edition as:

Weiss, John, 1944
    The advanced deer hunter's bible/by John Weiss : drawings by John F. Eggert.—1st ed.
        p.   cm.—(Doubleday outdoor bibles)
    ISBN 0-385-42351-9
    1. White-tailed deer hunting.   2. White-tailed deer.   I. Title.
SH301. W356   1993
799.2' 77357—dc20                     93-8180
                          CIP

ISBN 0-385-42351-9

19  18  17  16  15  14  13

# Table of Contents

Introduction  vii

1. The Whitetail's Eyes  9

2. Scents and Nonsense  19

3. The Whitetail's Ears  28

4. Reading a Deer's Body Language  35

5. Mapping out a Game Plan  44

6. Pellets, Tracks and Beds  54

7. Find the Food, Find the Deer  63

8. Antler Rubs Tell All  74

9. Analyzing the Rut  85

10. Scraping up a Buck  95

11. Rattle-in Your Buck  106

12. How Experts Call Deer  117

13. Decoy Your Deer  126

14. Weather and Whitetails  137

15. Stand and Blind Setups  148

16. Failsafe Stand and Blind Locations  157

17. The Art of Stillhunting  171

18. Advanced Drive Strategies  181

# Introduction

Recently, I was asked to give an after-dinner talk to a gathering of deer hunters at their organization's annual banquet. Generally such affairs are semiformal, and most speakers make their presentation rather brief.

This principle was further reinforced when, just before I was introduced, my host leaned over and whispered, "Don't talk above these people's heads and bore them with a lot of technicalities they probably won't understand."

But then a curious thing happened. At the conclusion of my talk I allowed for a question/answer period, and numerous hands instantly shot up.

The first question, from a young man who looked about twenty-five years old, was, "Can you explain how a buck deposits priming pheromones on antler rubs to induce does into an early estrus?"

The second question, from a woman in her mid-thirties, was, "When studying infrared aerial photographs through my stereoscope, why does the ground appear blue in places rather than brown or green?"

At that, I turned to my host and simply winked, for he had clearly underestimated this particular group of deer hunters, if not modern deer hunters in general.

As a postscript to this anecdote, it's worth saying that my talk that evening lasted approximately thirty minutes, yet the questions kept coming for an additional two hours before I felt a tickle developing in my throat and bid my guests goodnight.

A similar state of affairs has occurred with regards to the plethora of deer hunting books that have been released in the last several years. The majority of them describe at length how to sight-in a rifle, with accompanying drawings even showing where to aim at a deer should one pass by. And of course there are obligatory chapters on how to sharpen a knife and how to field-dress a deer.

Admittedly, such basics are useful to the newcomers to deer hunting who join our ranks each year. But vastly outnumbering them are the estimated 16 million others who are veterans of numerous deer seasons and who already have taken at least one or perhaps several decent bucks. A large percentage of these hunters have become quite sophisticated in their approach to deer hunting and thirst for the latest data from research biologists to help them better understand whitetail behavior.

It is for these serious hunters that *The Advanced Deer Hunter's Bible* has been written. I salute your love for whitetails and your unwavering dedication to the pursuit of North America's most popular big-game animal.

Kurt von Besser admires a spikehorn buck he took with a bow and arrow. Camo clothing helped him defeat the deer's keen eyesight.

# 1

## The Whitetail's Eyes

"Despite high-tech compound bows, scoped firearms, and other technological advances, only 12 percent of the nation's hunters succeed each year in taking a deer," my friend Kurt von Besser recently observed. "A pioneer who hunted as we do would have starved."

Yet venison was a regular part of the diets of our ancestors, which is especially remarkable considering that deer were far less plentiful then than now.

"Obviously, our forefathers had far more time to devote to hunting than does modern man," von Besser said. "But they also learned how to blend with the forest and thereby defeat the deer's keen visual abilities."

Savvy modern hunters can achieve the same end by wearing camouflage clothing that matches the color, tonal value and irregular shapes of the areas they hunt. If they are bowhunters, this means that just one camo outfit is not likely to serve the entire season. But even the gun hunter, who for safety reasons wants to be highly visible to other riflemen in the woods and thus wears blaze orange, can also adopt measures that will sharply reduce his visibility to deer.

### THE ULTRAVIOLET CONNECTION

Most are aware that for many decades virtually all fabric manufacturers have been putting ultraviolet pigments in their dyes so the colors will appear bold, bright and pleasing to the eye.

Similarly, on behalf of cleanliness-conscious housewives, manufacturers of nearly all laundry detergents these days add "optical brighteners" to their soap products. These chemicals leave an ultraviolet reflective residue on the fabric to further enhance the original u.v. color brightness dyes, which otherwise would tend to fade after repeated washings.

The significance of this to deer hunters is that biologists have recently discovered that animals such as deer have a unique visual apparatus which enables them to detect wavelengths of light deep into the blue end of the color spectrum, where ultraviolet light stands out boldly.

During the low-light hours of dawn and dusk, and after full dark, deer are able to see you.

In fact, it has been estimated that a whitetail deer's sensitivity to u.v. is at least 100 times more acute than that of humans. This means that at all times of day, but particularly during the low-light hours of dawn and dusk and after full dark, deer have the ability to see your clothing and identify your outline.

We now know why hunters have commonly experienced the frustration of having deer look squarely in their direction, apparently see something alarming and then instantly about-face and run away, even though they were dressed in full camo that matched their surroundings.

Of course, it's no longer a secret that deer can distinguish a wide range of colors. The revelation came about in 1977, at the U.S. Department of Agriculture's veterinary laboratory in College Station, Texas, where a team of biologists scientifically examined the eyes of live, anesthetized deer with electron microscopes.

They immediately detected the presence of a large number of nerve endings called "rods" in the deer's eyes, but this wasn't surprising. Rods are light receptors and they are plentiful in those animal species which commonly engage in nocturnal activities.

Therefore, it's understandable that deer should have a large number of rods to enable them to easily feed and move around in low-light conditions, and that in both darkness and daylight they should be quite adept at picking up the slightest movements to forewarn them of a predator on the prowl.

By comparison, humans don't have a high percentage of rods in their eyes, which explains why we possess poor night vision and why, even in broad daylight, slight movements around the periphery of our visual range often go unnoticed.

Next, the Texas biologists were surprised to discover a relatively high number of color-receptor "cones" in the deer's eyes. Humans have an abundance of cones, which allow them to distinguish even subtle shades of the same hue, so it stood to reason that deer might also have color vision capabilities.

The biologists then stimulated the eyes of the anesthetized deer with flashes of light spanning the entire range of the color spectrum, and the deer's cones duly responded to those lights in a manner almost identical to the way cones in human eyes involuntarily react. All of this provided the basic proof that deer do indeed possess the anatomical equipment (cones) for discerning colors and that it is indeed functional. It was then, in 1985, that a cooperative study of deer vision was undertaken between biologists at Michigan State University and the Michigan Department of Natural Resources.

While the Texas study had confirmed the presence of color vision anatomy in deer, and the functioning of that anatomy under laboratory conditions, the Michigan biologists wanted to test the operation of that color vision under natural conditions with deer fully awake.

They did this with penned deer, using standard conditioning techniques which entailed the offering of food rewards when the deer made correct responses to certain colors and by not rewarding them when their responses were incorrect.

As it happened, the deer had no trouble distinguishing between both long-wavelength and short-wavelength colors extending from one end of the color spectrum to the other. In fact—and this is startling—correct responses to the many different colors occurred as frequently as 95 percent of the time!

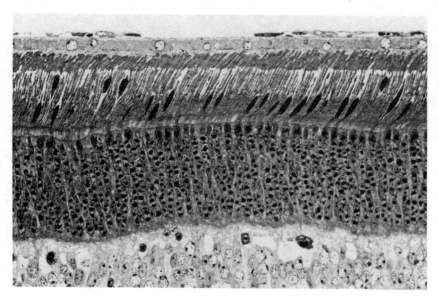

This electron-microscope photo, showing the presence of cones in a deer's eyes (the long, black cylinders), was the first evidence to confirm deer have color vision capabilities.

It was several years later, in 1989, that my regular hunting partner Kurt von Besser began studying color vision as well.

Von Besser is the honcho of ATSKO/Sno-Seal, the Orangeburg, South Carolina, company that in recent years has pioneered some of the most significant research in deer biology. And it was one particular experience Kurt had on a Montana deer hunt that virtually changed his life as a hunter.

"We were staying in a cabin and next to it, on a utility pole, was an ultraviolet bug light," Kurt explained. "Whenever we walked beneath this light after dark, our camo clothing took on a bright, blue-white glow just like a white shirt appears in a disco."

Since von Besser already was familiar with the color vision studies I mentioned earlier, he began seriously questioning how deer might perceive u.v. light. And, knowing that a Dr. Jay Neitz was currently involved in color vision research at the University of California, von Besser sought his help in filling in missing pieces of this growing jigsaw puzzle.

What von Besser learned shocked hunters nationwide and caused a revolution in the way camo clothing is now manufactured.

Dr. Neitz explained that as daylight fades, all creatures, including man and deer, depend more upon the rods in their eyes than their cones.

"The significance of this," Neitz said, "is that while cones are more responsive to long-wavelength colors at the red end of the color spectrum, rods are more responsive to the short-wavelength blue end of the spectrum."

If you've already guessed that u.v. light is found at the farthest, short-wavelength end of the spectrum, you're right! Therefore, what this means is that u.v. is the one color deer see best under all conditions but especially during low light levels!

Moreover, keep in mind, as mentioned earlier, that until just recently, all fabric dyes were loaded with u.v. chemicals which hunters and non-hunters have been further enhancing by using washing detergents to which still more u.v. brighteners are added.

## Why You Can't See Ultraviolet

Given all of the above, an obvious question is: Why can deer see ultraviolet light better than all other hues, but we humans can't?

One reason is because the eyes of deer are larger than those of humans, and their pupils can receive more light, including ultraviolet light, which activates their larger number of rods. Evidence that this occurs can be seen when a vehicle's headlights shine on a deer's eyes after dark. Their eyes glow bluish-green due to

Deer given food rewards were able to make correct color responses 95 percent of the time. Note this deer's glowing eyes. This is tapetum responding to ultraviolet light.

an anatomical feature called a tapetum at the rear of the eye.

Human eyes do not "shine" because light passes through the retina once and is absorbed at the back of the eye and lost forever. Yet, conversely, the deer's tapetum recycles the u.v. light back through the eye to reactivate the photoreceptors again and again, and it's this reflection we see in the headlights.

But even more crucial to u.v. vision, according to von Besser and Dr. Neitz, humans possess yellow filters in the lenses of their eyes. If we didn't have these anatomical devices to filter out u.v. light, images interpreted by our retinas would be slightly fuzzy and thereby limit our ability to see fine detail. This is why expert marksmen know they can improve their visual acuity by wearing yellow shooting glasses that block more short-wavelengths of light than the human lens alone is capable of blocking.

## Birth of U.V. Killer

Now you know why it's common to be perched high in a tree stand, remain totally motionless, with the wind in your favor, and yet see a deer come loping through the immediate area, suddenly slam to a halt, look squarely in your direction, and then vamoose!

Sure, millions of deer have been killed by hunters wearing camo clothing, but many other factors have likely contributed to their success by overriding the u.v. influence. Just one example might be the hunter whose stand is situated so that most of his body (and u.v. saturated garments) are hidden behind a tree trunk and his glowing camo is partly or completely blocked from view of the approaching deer.

Yet millions of still other deer have used their u.v. sensitivity to buy their tickets to freedom. As a result, most of the major manufacturers of hunting clothing have begun making major

When purchasing new camo clothing, look for hang-tags on garments to ensure they are not impregnated with u.v. dyes.

U.V. Killer is a blocking agent that can be used on clothing to prevent it from reflecting ultraviolet radiation.

**Always wash hunting clothes with a detergent that contains no optical brighteners. This brand, especially designed for hunters, also leaves garments entirely scent-free.**

**Hunter's trousers are untreated and reflect an ultraviolet glow that deer readily see. Jacket has been treated with U.V. Killer.**

changes. They are now requiring that the fabric mills which produce their bolts of camo cloth no longer add ultraviolet pigments to their dyes.

However, let's say your present selection of hunting garments, which you may have purchased several years ago and which almost surely contain u.v. pigments, still are in excellent condition and you don't want to throw them away and purchase entirely new clothing. The solution is easy!

When Kurt von Besser concluded his u.v. research, he immediately launched upon the development of a product he dubbed U.V. Killer, which is specifically designed to block u.v. radiation emitted by fabric dyes. U.V. Killer literally kills the shocking blue-white glow that is so easily spotted by deer and thereby allows your chosen camo pattern to blend with the natural cover of your surroundings.

Simply place your camo clothing (including hats, gloves, facemasks) on hangars and spray it with U.V. Killer. It dries completely scent-free within twenty-four hours.

Since there are always skeptics who scoff at such things, perform this easy experiment. Take an untreated article of clothing to a miniature golf course or any place where bug lights are turned on after dark and note how the clothing glows. Then treat the article with U.V. Killer and note the dramatic change. You've just succeeded in covering the reflective dye with a blocking dye.

Another revolutionary product is Sport-Wash, the only detergent advanced deer hunters now use. Sport-Wash is entirely scent free. Equally important, it is presently the only laundry detergent on the market that contains no optical brighteners and therefore leaves no u.v.

reflective residue on your garments. This is the detergent to use when you periodically need to launder camo clothing previously treated with U.V. Killer, to ensure that your clothing never again glows with u.v. radiation.

## THE BLAZE ORANGE FACTOR

Blaze orange is a proven safety color and therefore is now required during the firearm deer hunting seasons in most states. Simply put, blaze orange saves lives because a hunter wearing the bright color is highly visible to other hunters, particularly during the low-light hours of dawn and dusk when human vision is the least acute.

Yet many gun hunters, aware of the color

**Blaze orange is a proven safety color, but even when treated with U.V. Killer it is a solid block of uniform color that deer may detect.**

vision capabilities of deer, have come to believe that wearing blaze orange likewise makes them too conspicuous to deer as well, and that this hampers their chances of success. As a result, many of them don't wear orange and thus take unnecessary risks.

I suggest wearing an orange garment continuously while gun hunting. But hedge your bet by considering the use of "camo orange," which is simply blaze orange with an overlay of tree-branch designs to help your human body form better blend with your surroundings.

Also, of course, take advantage of the latest research findings and treat your garments with U.V. Killer and launder them only in Sport-Wash. U.V. Killer effectively blocks u.v. radiance at the lower wavelengths, yet leaves the orange brighteners intact in the upper wavelengths. As a result, the color is amuted yellow from the standpoint of how deer see it, yet it actually increases the visibility of blaze orange to the human eye.

## BOWHUNTING CAMO

Since the many camo "tree" patterns now available to hunters hadn't yet been conceived, our forefathers relied primarily upon checked patterns. Even today, red and black, and green and black, checked coats still are favorites among Northwoods deer hunters. Such patterns break up the hunter's form.

Then, following World War II, a profusion of mottled camo patterns came on the market, and they continue to be effective because in the outdoors there are seldom large uniform blocks of anything. Rather, the irregularity of the terrain itself, and the changing light intensities that play across equally irregular cover formations as clouds scud overhead, present everything to the eye as a hodgepodge of widely varied and disintegrated colors and tonal values. It should therefore be apparent that one essential of proper bowhunting camouflage is a mixture of light

Wearing proper bowhunting camouflage that incorporates light and dark tones, a hunter blends with the forest.

and dark tones that allows the hunter to melt into his surroundings.

If a bowhunter finds he is not as successful as he'd like to be in avoiding detection, it's probably necessary for him to fine-tune his selection of camo clothing. This requires some careful considerations. First, he must remember that the outdoors generally is more brightly illuminated during midday than at dawn and dusk. Moreover, the color and density of the cover itself changes dramatically as the season wears on. Consequently, a hunter who wants to sit in a tree stand deep in a hardwood forest early in the season might select a dark-green tree pattern with a floral overlay of light-green leaves. Yet two months later, in the very same location, he may prefer instead to wear a gray tree pattern with a dark-gray, gnarled branch overlay. Meanwhile, his partner stationed in a ground blind along the edge of a standing cornfield will undoubtedly want to wear a yellow/brown marshland camo pattern. Still later in the season, snow-covered ground dictates still another type of camo. Yet, contrary to what you might

**Contrary to popular belief, the best snow camo is not pure white but has an overlay of dark streaks to simulate shadows.**

how the rising sun is filtering through the cover and playing across the landscape to create long tentacles of shadows here and there and brightly illuminated places elsewhere. Then, and only then, do I allow my findings to dictate the exact tree for my stand and the type of clothing I'll wear."

Just one of many revolutionary clothing patterns now on the market which addresses these very concerns is called Bushlan (South Texas Camouflage, P.O. Box 73, Camp Verde, TX 78010). The uniqueness of Bushlan is that it was designed to be shape-disruptive at hunting distances near and far. Therefore, whether the deer is close or distant, the wearer

think, the most effective snow camo isn't pure white because in most instances snow is not brilliant white, even in direct sunlight. Rather, it has a muted gray tone, and this is why savvy hunters purchase snow camo with an overlay pattern of irregular gray or brown streaks.

My regular hunting partner Jeff Morris is such a fanatic about what we've just described here that he uses a unique pre-season scouting plan that I've since adopted myself.

"After I've thoroughly canvassed the terrain, evaluated all existing sign, and determined the general area where I want to install my stand, I then decide whether the place should best be hunted during the morning or evening," Jeff explained. "If it's to be an early-morning stand, I'll return early the next morning to see exactly

**When selecting a stand site, consider the angle of the sun. Then get back into the shade so that if a deer looks in your direction he'll be staring into bright light and won't be able to see you in your camo clothing.**

Biologist Larry Weishuhn: "The Bushlan camo pattern we developed is three-dimensional and even allows a hunter to move slowly about without being seen."

appears as part of his background rather than as a solid blob.

According to my friend Larry Weishuhn, a deer biologist who helped design Bushlan, "We've achieved a three-dimensional appearance through the use of certain colors not found in other camo clothing. For example, in between our realistic leaf and stem design is the color yellow to closely simulate the 3-D effect of sunlight shining on the outer limbs and leaves of vegetation. Yet the yellow, along with other colors, has a chameleon effect when the hunter is in shaded areas of cover. This concept is a first in the development of camo because it actually allows a hunter to move around (slowly!) with far less chance of being detected."

# 2

# Scents and Nonsense

Biologists say the olfactory center of a deer's brain, which absorbs odor molecules the deer is continually monitoring, is 10,000 times more well developed than man's and that deer are able to distinguish between six different odors at the same time.

Commercial scents for deer hunters have proliferated, but not without much attending controversy. Are the companies that sell various elixirs simply snake-oil salesmen attempting to flimflam gullible deer hunters? Or is there any validity to the use of scents?

I've seen many types of scents work, both for me and others. And in countless cases, those other hunters haven't merely been armchair talkers but have acquired reputations for taking some of the biggest bucks in their regions. Some of those hunters, in fact, are university biologists and researchers employed by the largest and most respected manufacturers of deer scents.

One such hunter worth mentioning here is Dr. Greg Bambenek, of Duluth, Minnesota, whom I hunted with last year. Bambenek is the founder of the Osmic Research Company, which has been at the forefront in analyzing the

The part of a deer's brain that analyzes odors is 10,000 times more well developed than man's. That's why I use various scents, to level the playing field.

Dr. Greg Bambenek: "A deer's olfactory system is a closed loop independent of conscious thought, which allows it to react immediately without forethought."

roles various odors play in deer communication. And since Bambenek is a licensed M.D., who intently examines deer scents from a highly scientific viewpoint, it stands to reason his investigations are based upon solid evidence, not advertising hype.

"In the sensory world of deer, hearing and vision are crucial to functioning in their environments, but there is evidence their sense of smell is far more important," Dr. Bambenek told me. "You see, hearing and vision require thought processes, mental interpretation and mutual confirmation. But a deer's olfactory system is independent of conscious discrimination. It is a closed loop because, like a knee jerk reflex, a scent signal leads to immediate action without forethought."

But which particular category of scents are bucks most likely to respond to positively and which negatively?

"Well, metatarsal scent is definitely an alarm pheromone," Bambenek said. "This is the scent deer release from their metatarsal glands to warn other nearby deer of danger, as when they've encountered a dog or when a hunter suddenly surprises them at close range. So be sure to smell every scent you buy. If you ever find one that has a distinct garlic odor, that company didn't do any research and included metatarsal gland secretions. Don't throw the scent away, however, because it can be used as a very effective trail block to divert deer traffic in a different direction."

What about urine-based scents, and especially those brands advertised as containing doe-in-heat urine?

"My own research has confirmed that urine-based scents often have a reverse effect," Dr. Bambenek answered. "Ninety percent of the year, the scent of a doe in estrus does not make any sense to a male deer. And estrus scents certainly are not attractive to does because they do not want to be mistaken for females in heat and have bucks chase them all over when they are not receptive."

Noted naturalist Leonard Lee Rue III is in complete agreement. In his book *Whitetail Hunting,* Rue is very specific:

"Estrous urine lures used before the buck begins making his scrapes will probably spook him rather than attract him," Rue states. "And sex lures used more than three weeks before, or anytime after, the doe reaches estrus will spook her. They may attract a random buck, but when does spook from the untimely scent and leave the area, the bucks go with them."

## PULLING DEER TO YOU

With this insight, Dr. Juice Deer Attractant was Greg Bambenek's solution (no pun intended) to most deer hunters' woes, for the approach is based entirely upon natural deer communication.

"The oil of the tarsal gland, not urine, is the key to attracting deer," Bambenek claims.

The tarsal glands are large, hair-covered slits located just above the knee joint on the insides of each hind leg. They remain open to the air and constantly emit scent which uniquely identifies each animal, just like human fingerprints, thus enabling deer to recognize members of their local herd as well as strangers.

"Any quality scent containing tarsal gland secretions is a hunter's best bet," Bambenek believes, "simply because it is effective for both bucks and does and it works throughout the entire hunting season."

Moreover, since Dr. Juice Deer Attractant, specifically, is based upon the tarsal scent of both North American and foreign deer, it stimulates an intense curiosity and territorial response in the biological language of odor that deer constantly use.

In fact, Bambenek's field researchers have reported seeing bucks closely following does and leaving the does when they smelled the tarsal odor of Dr. Juice Deer Attractant, and perhaps interpreted it as a foreign challenger that had recently come into the region.

Bambenek has discovered that, because of both the territorial response and the curiosity response which is elicited by this particular scent, it is not only ideal for stand hunting but also for grunting, antler rattling and decoying.

"If you combine the use of a grunt call or rattling antlers with a tarsal attractant scent and a decoy, it's possible to create a fail-safe illusion," Greg Bambenek explains. "You'll trigger the buck's sense of hearing with the calling effort. With the scent you'll convince him there is another deer in the immediate region, which

Most experts concede that tarsal scent, not urine-based scent, is the key to attracting deer.

Greg Bambenek: "A tarsal scent that is derived from both North American and foreign deer stimulates curiosity and a territorial response."

may be either a local deer or an intruder, depending upon how he interprets the odor. And when he arrives to investigate, he'll be able to see that another deer has indeed ventured into his domain. From that point on, whether or not you succeed in taking him really only depends upon how well you've placed your stand and how well practiced you are with your chosen firearm or bow."

## SEASON OF THE RUT

Despite Greg Bambenek's opinion that urine-based lures are ineffective, other authorities look at the subject from a slightly different perspective.

"During the rut, a doe's estrous urine is precisely what attracts amorous males," says Linda Robbins Leascher. Leasher's father founded the famous Robbins Scent Company, which is

By combining proper camouflage, antler rattling, a quality scent and perhaps a decoy, you can defeat all three of a deer's senses.

based in Pennsylvania and maintains its own captive herd of over 400 deer. "Admittedly, however, no company can market a 100 percent estrous urine product. Since urine is basically ammonia, it will ferment, whereby its chemical composition changes, if not stabilized with a preservative. So be wary of any company that says their scent is pure deer urine."

The Robbins Scent Company doesn't try to second-guess when their does will come into estrus. Rather, they believe that anytime during mid-October through February at least 25 percent or more of their does will be in some stage of their estrous cycle and this will be reflected as estorus secretions in their urine. Therefore, since the urine is mixed after having been collected, it will be at least 25 percent estrus in content.

While some animal scientists disagree as to whether tarsal scent or estrous urine is more effective, other individuals are taking the middle of the road and using both. One is noted deer biologist Dr. James Kroll, a professor at Stephen F. Austin University, who also heads deer management programs on many large Texas ranches. In a nutshell, Kroll states that "hock glands from rutting bucks are the only scent aids I've used with positive results. That's because bucks engage in a procedure known as rub-urinating in which they squeeze their hind legs together, hunch up their backs and then urinate over their tarsal glands."

Particularly when rattling and using grunt calls during the rut, the combination of the urine and tarsal odor carried by the air conveys the message to a responding buck that other male deer are in the vicinity, prompting him to want to investigate to determine the status of the situation.

Tarsal glands can be collected from bucks that you and your partners take. To preserve them for future use, store them in your freezer

**Bucks and does alike deposit tarsal gland scent throughout their home ranges as a means of communicating their presence to each other.**

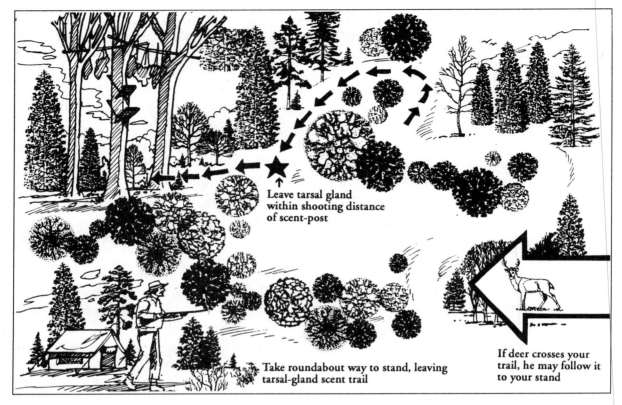

Leave tarsal gland
within shooting distance
of scent-post

Take roundabout way to stand, leaving
tarsal-gland scent trail

If deer crosses your
trail, he may follow it
to your stand

Tie a tarsal gland to your boot before hiking to your stand, and if a
buck crosses your trail he may follow you right to your stand.

in plastic bags with zip-loc closures. Later, tie a gland to your boot so that it drags on the ground while hiking to your stand and then remove it and hang it from a nearby branch; if a buck crosses the trail you've laid down, he may be inclined to follow it right to your location.

## THE BIG COVER-UP

"If a hunter insists upon buying and using only one type of scent," Linda Robbins Leascher advises, "I don't think he should use some type of attractant or lure. The effectiveness of these scents is limited to certain applications during a brief period each year. Much smarter would be for him to use some type of cover scent." Linda did not advise a specific type of cover scent made by her company because some types may work under certain conditions and others won't.

The key is learning how to identify those predominant odors in the region you're planning to hunt and then duplicating those odors on your person so that you fit in like a piece of the forest's woodwork. In using specific types of cover scents in their proper context, the hunter will soon discover that an apple scent near an apple orchard can be his ticket to success. Yet in a pine plantation or swampy riverbottom, where there are no apple trees, that very same apple scent may cost him the buck of a lifetime.

I believe still other masking scents are ineffective everywhere and under all conditions.

Take skunk scent, for example, which I believe actually decreases a hunter's chances of seeing deer. Contrary to the claims made by some scent companies, skunk scent is not a common woodland odor that deer encounter regularly and automatically accept as a natural component of their habitat.

I live and work in a rural area where skunks are plentiful, and when we infrequently detect skunk odor in the air it is so pungently uncharacteristic it rivets our attention in the direction from which it is coming. Surely, that sudden odor-oddity draws the notice of deer as well.

Therefore, common sense tells us that a hunter who sprinkles skunk scent around his stand is not melting into the outdoors. Rather, he is standing out just as boldly as if he turned on sirens and flashing lights to pinpoint his location.

Moreover, keep in mind that every creature in the animal kingdom has a method of exhibiting a fear response, and skunks are no exception. When a skunk sprays its repellent as a means of self-defense, it is telling all the world that it is alarmed. The reason could be a pack of free-roaming dogs or coyotes that have cornered it, or a wolf or cougar in wilderness regions, or even a human that unexpectedly happened upon the animal at close range. In any event, these potential threats to skunks are the very same ones that deer have learned to avoid since they were fawns. They even may have had close calls in which the air suddenly was filled with rank skunk odor and moments later a hungry predator came bounding through the woodlands.

The point is that since skunks release their odor as a self-defense mechanism, there is no way for a deer to make any kind of positive association with the scent. There is no way it can be recognized, interpreted, or accepted as "normal." On the contrary, if a whitetail detects skunk odor, its previous conditioning dictates

If possible, keep your hunting clothes outdoors in fresh breezes. If it's necessary to bring them indoors, stow them in plastic bags so they don't absorb household odors.

that its response will be negative.

So ask yourself, do you really want skunk scent on your clothing or near your stand, even if a manufacturer's claim that it hides human odor is true? Perhaps the same could even be said of fox urine or many other scent variations on the market.

As an advanced hunter striving for a high plateau of deer hunting expertise, take the time to think such matters through. Meanwhile, never lose sight of the fact that a whitetail's very survival hinges upon the deer's ability to detect anything that is not a usual and customary part of its environment. So there is little value in attempting to hide your odor if you simply replace it with something that is equally out of place and therefore elicits a fear response.

## DISAPPEAR IN PLAIN SIGHT

Many hunters nowadays try to go afield as odor-free as possible. Many of them have doubts about the use of deer scents and are perplexed as to why the animals react favorably to some scents and yet spook at others. Since many such mysteries may never be unlocked, they've decided to eliminate the scent factor altogether.

This new attitude is being addressed by a number of innovative chemists who have intensively studied the subject of odors and designed some revolutionary products for hunters.

In healthy people, sweat released by the apocrine glands has no immediate odor. The odor is the result of normal bacterial growth. This skin bacteria, when exposed to the air, emits a gas, and it's the gas which is odoriferous. Therefore, if you eliminate the existing bacteria, and prevent its speedy recurrence, you eliminate deer-alarming man scent.

Trouble is, a majority of bath soaps on the market are either perfumed or contain lanolin, cold cream, cocoa butter, or some other fragrance. So once again, you're simply replacing your human odor with something else that is equally out of place. Much better is bathing with Sport-Wash Unscented Hair & Body Soap, or even Phisoderm (which is the soap hospitals use to eliminate skin bacteria before patients undergo surgery).

Also remember that the body's natural production of skin bacteria never ceases, so you'll want to bathe just prior to leaving home or camp; if you bathe the evening before, your body will have eight hours to farm a bumper

N-O-DOR is literally a shower in a bottle. Intended for in-field use during hot weather, it refreshes and cleans you in minutes.

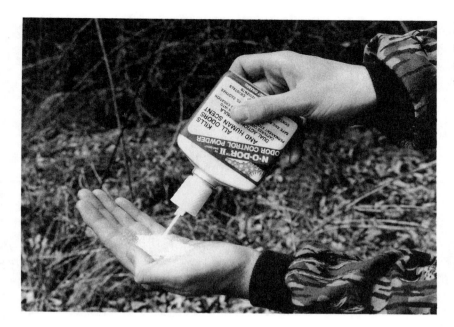

N-O-DOR II in dry powder form is the answer to total odor removal in cold weather.

crop of new bacteria before you find yourself in the deer woods the following morning.

Equally defeating is slipping into hunting garments which have become impregnated with all manner of perfumes found in most laundry detergents. Better is to use scent-free Sport-Wash Detergent, or Arm & Hammer Baking Soda Detergent, then hang your duds outdoors to dry in fresh breezes. When the clothes are dry, stow them in plastic bags so they are not subjected to household odors or leave them outdoors in an open-air shed.

Next, a hunter will want to ensure that after many hours of prolonged exertion afield he doesn't once again begin exuding human odors that are sure to alarm deer. This is of special concern to hunters setting up a base of operations in a tent camp or remote cabin where regular bathing is not possible or practical.

Once again my friend Kurt von Besser, honcho of ATSKO/Sno-Seal, has come to the rescue with a fully researched product called N-O-DOR.

"There are numerous scent-eliminating sprays on the market," von Besser admits, "but most are only 3 percent baking soda solutions that merely absorb odors for brief periods of time."

Yet N-O-DOR actually destroys all odors at the molecular level through the process of oxidation. When you're on stand and beginning to feel sweaty and grungy, or back in camp after many hours of stillhunting, simply unbutton your shirt, loosen your belt and spray your bare skin. Be sure to give special attention to areas where perspiration and related body odor are the first to appear, such as the face, scalp, underarms, groin, small of the back, and behind the knees. There is no need to dry off. Now, button up, zip up, and for several hours you will feel totally refreshed and squeaky clean, just as if you stepped out of a shower. More important, you will no longer be releasing human scent into the air for deer to smell.

If the weather is too cold to use a liquid spray, use the companion product N-O-DOR II in dry powder form. Just dust your body with several handfuls and once again you'll instantly be scent-free for up to twelve hours; after that, dust yourself again for continuing scent-free hunting.

In coming chapters, we'll have more to say about the use of both scents and scent-free hunting as they apply to stand placement and especially to hunting during the rut.

# 3

## The Whitetail's Ears

Most hunters focus their attention on outwitting a deer's nose and its keen eyesight. But a whitetail's ears are also keen sense organs. Of course, there is a big difference between what a deer hears and classifies as normal and what is likely to alarm it.

The brushy hollows, cedar swamps, juniper flats, hardwood ridges, riverbottom thickets, pine plantations and other places where deer live are seldom very serene. But this should come as no surprise to those who have spent long hours sitting unobtrusively in the woods as the outdoor world gradually became oblivious to their presence and resumed its normal course of activity.

Songbirds emit a continual cacophony of sounds ranging from musical chirpings to harsh, scolding notes as they flit from bush to branch and play tag through an overhead umbrella of cover. Incessantly chattering squirrels rustle in the fallen wardrobe of autumn, and when high in the limbs vigorously shake the outermost extremities of leafy branches as they search for and pluck acorns. In good squirrel country there may seem to be an almost contin-

ual rain of cuttings from above. In various regions, turkeys, black bears, javelinas, armadillos and a host of other creatures may similarly share a deer's home range and contribute their own unique sounds.

There are numerous non-animal noises that permeate the places where bucks and does live. The wind whistles and clacks together the limbs of close-standing trees. Hollow sounds punctuate the stillness as black walnuts or the fruits of the osage orange fall to the earth with distinct thuds. There are the clinking noises of rolling gravel on ever-shifting talus slopes, and the disturbances of tumbling rocks and boulders loosened by time and eroding weather. Brooks and streams bubble, lightning cracks, thunder pounds and once-mighty oaks fall with great crashes.

Indeed, the outdoor world is a very noisy place, and every day deer are bombarded by hundreds of such stimuli which their ears must sift through and evaluate.

A deer's ability to catalog sounds is both incredible and unfailingly accurate. For example, I frequently hunt the fringe areas of hilly

A whitetail's ears have a reflective surface of 24 inches and can swivel 180 degrees.

southern Ohio where a common farming practice is called woods-pasturing, and it is not unusual to see a cow actually walk by my deer stand. The intriguing thing about this is that in the brushy hollows, stands of saplings and other cover, cows make a variety of noises. Yet deer in the area, even though they can hear the cattle but often cannot see them, seldom pay the livestock any mind. Perhaps it is the unique way in which cattle or other stock move, with a certain rhythm or cadence to the footfalls. But just let the farmer or rancher quietly walk into the area to check his stock or count heads, and the deer are immediately aware of his presence and soon thereafter are usually gone.

## HOW DEER HEAR

Just how keen is a whitetail's sense of hearing?

Scientific studies with penned deer have revealed they have very brief attention spans of about three minutes.

When you break a dry twig or make some other noise, come to an immediate halt for at least five minutes. By then, nearby deer will have forgotten the sound.

Well, it is particularly acute for distinguishing high-pitched sounds extending to 30,000 cycles per second. By comparison, our human hearing range extends to only 16,000 cycles per second.

Additionally, each of a deer's ears has an enormous reflective surface of 24 square inches and can swivel in a 180-degree arc. By comparison, our ears encompass only about 3½ square inches and cannot be swiveled.

On detecting sounds, deer behave the same as humans by engaging in the three-step process of recognition, classification and response. Also like us, depending upon the nature of the first two elements, the third element—response—may entail no behavioral reaction whatever.

## The Doppler Effect

An interesting aspect of a whitetail's hearing process has to do with the variable distances at which deer are capable of detecting those particular sounds they are most likely to respond to. Scientists call this the Doppler Effect.

Picture yourself standing along a roadside and seeing a semi truck approaching in the distance. The driver simultaneously sees you and

A whitetail's curiosity sometimes causes him to throw caution to the wind. This buck couldn't resist investigating a squirrel call.

as a warning signal gives a long, continual blast on his air horn. As the truck draws nearer and nearer, the pitch of the horn seems to rise. When the truck passes, the pitch begins dropping until the truck fades into the distance and you can no longer hear it.

You've just experienced the Doppler Effect. As the truck approached closer and closer, the horn's sound waves became compressed or crowded close together, causing a type of upheaval in the number of cycles per second of vibration reaching your ear, which your brain translated into a higher pitch. Then, after the truck passed, the sound waves became stretched out or gradually spaced wider and wider apart, with fewer and fewer cycles per second of vibration reaching your ear with a resulting lower pitch. Actually, the pitch of the air horn never changed at all, only your perception of that pitch in accordance with the varying distances at which the sound was heard.

From an anatomical standpoint, whitetails "hear" in the same manner as humans. But because the neural channels linking their ears to their brains are attuned to much higher-pitched sounds than we are capable of discerning, they tend to overreact to those noises occurring closest to them, which may not necessarily be "loud" noises but are characterized by higher numbers of cycles per second. This is understandable because the closest noises are the very ones most likely to influence the effectiveness with which members of the same species are able to communicate with each other.

To illustrate this important point, you may be watching a doe and notice with surprise that she doesn't react at all to the crack of a distant gunshot, a sound that immediately drew your notice, but she'll instantly turn her head in the direction of her nearby fawn at its faintest mewing for attention. I've also seen a buck beneath my stand exhibit no alarm reaction whatever to the clearly audible, laughing voices

of several farmhands mending fences in the distance. But then, at the barely discernible sound of clearing my throat twelve feet away, the buck dashed off.

## They Can't Remember!

Interestingly, however, a deer doesn't always bolt upon hearing a sound that may ultimately prove harmful. The animal may be unable to pinpoint the exact source or location of the sound and will freeze and cup its ears. Its eyes go to work as well, trying to spot movements that may be associated with whatever made the sound.

Studies involving the presentation of various types of stimuli to penned deer have shown that the animals possess sensory attention spans of various lengths. Incidents of the moment that

Obviously alert, yet with their curiosity overriding their usual wariness, these does were intrigued by the author's turkey calls.

trigger their senses of vision or smell may cause whitetails to remain alert for quite a while. And when these two senses are alerted simultaneously, or when one quickly follows the other, the animal predictably shifts into high gear to leave the area as quickly as possible. Yet in the absence of confirmation from the other senses, the chink in a whitetail's armor is a very short memory. Scientists say it's limited to about three minutes.

All of this means that you don't have to worry too much about the sounds you make. Not only are they inevitable, but in typical whitetail habitat they constitute only a small percentage of the numerous other sound-stimuli that bombard deer every hour of every day. Just remember to stop when you snap a twig or crunch dry leaves underfoot and don't even blink an eyelid for four to five minutes. Then you can begin slowly advancing once again, with the confidence that any deer in the vicinity that heard your initial sound have now forgotten it and returned their attention to feeding or other activities.

Once in South Carolina's Francis Marion National Forest, I was sneaking through a lowland swamp when I spotted a six-point buck about 150 yards ahead of me. As I began raising my rifle, my jacket sleeve grated against the rough bark of a cypress branch, and the deer immediately turned and looked squarely in my direction. I almost stopped breathing. Long minutes later, the deer continued ambling along, browsing upon branch tips drooping from willow saplings. I took only one step forward to improve my shooting position and then silently cursed when my boot made a loud sucking noise as I pulled it out of the swamp muck. Again the deer wheeled around and gave me the once-over, craning his head from one side to the other. Fortunately, the wind was in my favor and surrounding brush adequately broke up my outline. Finally, the deer continued nibbling on the tender willow twigs, and

this time I managed to center my crosshairs on his shoulder and drop him.

## IT'S A DEER'S WORLD

In going back to my earlier mention of how noisy whitetail habitat can be at times, and the ability of deer to catalog sounds, it's worth repeating that deer become intimately familiar with the sounds that characterize their own particular home ranges.

I remember being stationed at Ft. Benning, Georgia, for example, and seeing deer placidly grazing not far from the artillery range where the sounds of impacting mortar and bazooka shells were deafening. Anywhere else, deer would have undoubtedly charted nonstop courses for the next county, but here they had grown used to the everyday training exercises of infantrymen.

Near where we used to live in Florida, armadillos were as thick as flies. They would root around noisily in dense stands of palmetto, while nearby deer ignored them. In Texas, I've often sat in tower blinds and watched javelinas bickering among themselves as they rustled around in mesquite and prickly pear. I could see them although nearby deer couldn't, and yet the deer seemed to register no alarm whatever. In other areas, the sounds of chainsaws used by logging crews or of farm machinery in agricultural regions may not bother deer. Such sounds are not alien to their environment.

In monitoring the sounds in their environments, whitetails seem able to interpret the alarm signals of other creatures. Just a few examples are the scolding bark of gray and fox squirrels, the shrill scream of the jay, the raucous warning call of the crow, and the "putt" of the turkey. The savvy hunter tries not to alert other creatures, for they may turn on their own warning sirens.

Finally, I'd like to relate two anecdotes that illustrate the curiosity whitetails sometimes display when it comes to sounds they've obviously never heard before.

I had been reading a book on small-game hunting in which the author recommended loudly kissing the back of your hand to bring shy squirrels out of hiding. On my next bushy-tail outing I tried it, and an eight-point buck sneaked into view, apparently trying to find the source of the sound.

Another time I tried my skill at handcrafting a turkey call I'd read about. As it happened, the high-pitched squeal the call made was absolutely horrible and sounded nothing like any turkey I'd ever heard. I decided to field-test it anyway. To my amazement, two does, mesmerized by the bizarre noise, approached to within five yards of my position, then detected me and bounded away.

Such is the spontaneous and unpredictable behavior of whitetails.

# 4

# Reading a Deer's Body Language

I was about ready to concede defeat. For six days I had watched a scrape-littered trail without seeing as much as a chipmunk, and now Ohio's 1991 deer season was rapidly drawing to a close. Then a big doe sauntered into view.

"Well, I sure was hoping for a hefty set of antlers," I muttered under my breath, "but you'll make many fine meals."

As it happened, however, I never did squeeze the trigger on that doe because just as my scope's crosshairs began settling on her lung region I noticed she was holding her tail cocked off to one side, and I knew what that meant. Moments later, an impressive eight-point buck came loping down the very same trail. This time, I felt the stock of the slug-loaded shotgun pound my shoulder. Then I felt immense satisfaction because my countless years of studying whitetail behavior, and learning to interpret their body language, had paid off handsomely. I've often wondered how many other hunters, finding themselves in precisely the same situation, would have taken the doe for freezer venison without the slightest realization that a nice buck was about to step into view.

## RUT POSTURING BEHAVIOR

As humans, we communicate thoughts and intentions through the use of a wide variety of unspoken gestures and body postures. For those who are hearing impaired, we even have an entire system of communication based upon hand movements alone. If a hunter learns to decode the messages that deer exchange, he can significantly increase his ability to assimilate and successfully react to all types of hunting situations.

In the experience I described above, the doe was holding her tail cocked off to one side in the universal go-ahead signal a female deer employs to tell a buck trailing slightly behind that she has approached the zenith of her estrous cycle and is receptive to being bred. If a doe ever comes by your stand exhibiting this specific body posture, get ready for action! In brief minutes, you should find yourself

**A dominant buck prances proudly with his head held high and his tail extended and tilted down at the tip.**

rewarded with a shot at a sexed-up buck who is so intent upon closing the distance to the doe that he'll be oblivious to your presence.

During the rutting period, bucks likewise send messages with their tails. Across most of the range inhabited by whitetails, as many as a dozen male deer may find themselves sharing the same home turf, and they adhere to well-defined pecking orders. Within this hierarchal ranking the so-called alpha buck, which maintains dominance over all the younger subordinate deer, commonly saunters around with his head held high and his tail extended straight back and tilted slightly down at the very tip.

This is intimidating body language, and lesser deer quickly learn to respect the dominant buck's authority, for to do otherwise is to risk a charge and possible antler goring. Subordinate males display their respect in the presence of a superior male by walking timidly with a rather stiff-legged gait and a swaybacked posture, holding the head low and the tail tucked between their legs, and avoiding eye contact.

If, for example, a hunter spots a 2½-year-old eight-point buck coming in his direction, displaying submissive behavior, he might elect to let the deer go about his business. Although the buck may indeed be a very nice one, his behavior indicates he's actually quite low in social ranking and that there's a much larger buck on the prowl in the immediate vicinity.

## HEAD-BOBBING

Other mannerisms can be equally revealing. The most common behavior in this category is known as head-bobbing, which males and females alike engage in when they sense danger.

Freeze! This buck is head-bobbing in an attempt to trick you into moving so he can determine your location. If you even flinch, he's gone.

A doe standing perfectly motionless for long periods of time is alarmed. Other deer seeing this posture will also become alert.

**Buck exhibiting Flehmen posture with head held high and upper lip curled back. This deer has detected a pleasurable odor in the air and would like to find its source.**

In making the head-bobbing maneuver, the deer typically begins to lower its head toward the ground as if to feed but then quickly jerks its head back up. This sudden, unexpected movement can cause a predator or hunter to flinch and thereby reveal his presence. If you fall for this age-old trick, you've blown your cover and probably won't have a shot unless it's a hurried one at a rapidly departing animal.

In conjunction with head-bobbing, a suspicious deer may also periodically crane its neck from side to side, as if to change its visual perspective. It may also stamp its front feet, which is both an attempt to force a response from whatever is near and to warn other nearby deer of impending danger.

If the deer stops stamping its feet and alternately craning its head left and right, and lowers its head and actually begins feeding, take the opportunity to raise your bow or gun for the shot; the deer has convinced itself no harm lurks nearby.

It's also worth noting that bucks and does frequently spend long periods of time completely motionless. A motionless doe is a nervous doe,

and all other deer in the vicinity that see her exhibiting this posture, with her tail down and still, will go on radar-alert. Then, when she becomes convinced no danger is imminent, she will begin flicking her tail as a signal that she's about to move a few more steps forward or resume feeding.

Bucks remain perfectly motionless for long moments in order to survey their surroundings and watch the behavior of other deer in the vicinity. They do not do this because they are spooked but simply because they are ultra cautious.

So keep in mind that in whitetail body language, a motionless doe is always a suspicious and jittery deer that is distrustful of what is ahead, but a motionless buck is just being his usual self.

## ODORS ON THE WIND

In addition to visual means of communication, deer also rely on their other senses from time to time. One of the most notable types of behavior is the "Flehman response," named after the biologist who first identified it.

This deer has smelled something alarming. The clue is the tongue protruding out of the side of the mouth. Note also the ears folded back in pre-flight response. Maybe your deer scent is scaring him?

When a buck exhibits Flehman behavior, it holds its head high and tilted back while simultaneously opening its mouth and curling its upper lip back so the gums show. This posture, which exposes the vomeronasal organ at the back of the palate to a maximum amount of air, is used to decipher the exact nature of a pleasurable odor the deer has detected so that he can locate its source.

Most Flehman behavior occurs when a buck detects a faint whiff of estrous doe odor. However, bucks and does alike also exhibit Flehman behavior in response to a wide variety of other odors they cannot identify, which may include commercial deer scents used by hunters.

Just the opposite occurs when a deer smells something very strange, out of place, or alarming. Now, the animal drops its head low, to about knee level, and protrudes its tongue laterally out of the side of its mouth. Quite often, the negative odor the deer has detected is human scent, but it can also be a commercial deer scent in the wrong environment. For example, I have seen deer register alarm on detecting a pine cover scent in a region where there were no pine trees, or a doe-in-heat scent during the non-rutting period.

## WATCH THEIR EARS

The deer woods are actually quite noisy places, but there is a world of difference between what a deer hears and what a deer hears that frightens it. As a result, deer have developed an uncanny ability to catalog what they hear as normal, versus other sounds that may place their hides in jeopardy.

Many times I've seen a deer cup both ears and point them in a particular direction, indicating it heard something in the distance and is listening for follow-up sounds. Quite often, when I've seen deer engage in this behavior, they have then turned and bolted for no apparent reason. But then, five or ten minutes later, I've seen another hunter come poking along through the woodlands.

It's also quite common for deer to periodically swivel their ears in different directions.

**With ears cupped forward, this buck is listening intently to a sound he has heard up ahead.**

They can aim one ear forward and the other directly to the rear, enabling them to hear sounds coming from entirely different directions. When a hunter observes a deer engaging in this behavior, he can presume the deer is uneasy because his sense of hearing has been triggered by something approaching from his rear. That "something" may be another hunter sneaking along, several hunters staging a drive, or even a dog trailing the deer.

Paying close attention to the way a doe holds her ears can enable a smart hunter to take a buck. If a doe has one ear pointed forward and the other cupped to the rear as she minces along, she's simultaneously checking for anything that might be up ahead along her intended travel route and listening for sounds on her backtrail. During the earliest weeks of the hunting season, she's undoubtedly keeping tabs on twin fawns following behind. But if it's November, December or January, an enterprising hunter knows the doe has by now chased her fawns away in order to engage in breeding and that it's highly probable a rutting buck is

**With one ear pointing forward and the other cupped to the rear, this buck reveals the whitetail's amazing ability to monitor simultaneously sounds coming from different directions.**

This small buck has just stepped into a clearing to feed and has now turned to look over his shoulder. Be patient. Another deer is following him, and you may eventually be rewarded with a shot at a much larger animal.

Shoot quickly! This deer has sensed danger in the vicinity and folded his ears back in preparation for escape.

following her. Don't even blink!  Let her pass unaware of your presence and rivet your attention on her backtrail.

When a deer is monitoring something following behind, it will of course frequently turn its head and look over its shoulder. If, for example, a doe or small buck steps from a forest edge into an open meadow to feed and then occasionally looks back over its shoulder, a savvy hunter will wait for a much larger buck to make an appearance.

Yet if a buck or doe suddenly lays both ears back, you've been had. The insides of a white-tail's ears are very sensitive, and the animals fold them back just before fleeing so they won't be stung by briars and thorny brambles when they bound away through brush cover. If you observe this behavior, you might as well take your best shot because in moments the deer will be gone. An exception to this rule is when a buck lays its ears back, lowers its head and bristles the hair on the back of its neck. This buck is extremely agitated and is displaying a very aggressive posture toward another buck you may not yet be able to see in nearby cover.

## WHITE FLAGS WAVING

Most hunters know that spooked deer usually run with their tails held high and waving from side to side. However, this type of body language is far more characteristic of does than of bucks. Because a deer's gray/brown coloration blends well with its surroundings, it would be easy for a mature doe in flight to lose her offspring, leaving them vulnerable to predators. As

**A buck waving his tail as he flees. Does nearly always "flag," especially if accompanied by fawns, but the behavior is rare among bucks.**

a result, a doe intentionally "flags" because the flash of the waving white tail is like a neon sign to her yearling fawns. It guides her offspring when they follow her through dense and dark cover as she dodges left or right and bounds over obstacles.

Conversely, bucks take no responsibility for rearing their offspring and therefore do not instinctively "flag" when running. When they do indeed occasionally wave their tails, it is merely a happenstance.

If you jump several deer from heavy cover and they bound away, it's often quite difficult to determine which animal is a buck. But if you focus your attention upon the animal that has not lofted a waving white flag and note if it has antlers, your sights will settle on the only buck in the group.

When deer are not in the process of fleeing but are simply going about business routinely, the manner in which they move their tails is equally informative.

For example, if a deer looks squarely in your direction, don't automatically presume the animal has spotted you. This is when many novice hunters commit the cardinal error of thinking they have been detected and that they might as well raise their gun or bow. Then, their movement does indeed give away their location, and the deer bounds away. Yet if the hunter had remained perfectly motionless, he might have ultimately been awarded a shot at a totally unsuspecting animal.

The key to pulling this off is watching the animal's tail and interpreting what it is thinking. If the tail remains down and occasionally swishes from side to side, rest assured the deer has the peace of mind that he is in no danger, which means you've got plenty of time to wait for the perfect shot. But if the deer looks in your direction, suddenly raises its tail and extends it straight backward, the jig is up and you might as well take your best shot. This is an alarmed animal that has made up his mind to vamoose.

However, keep in mind it's always necessary to relate your interpretation of deer body language to the immediate circumstances. I've often seen deer coming toward me, holding their tails straight back, but this alarm reaction was not in response to my presence. They were actually fleeing from other hunters far in the distance and had no idea I was waiting up ahead. Remember, too, that bucks commonly extend their tails straight back to intimidate subordinate bucks, and just prior to defecating.

We know that a human being's body language often speaks more clearly than words. The same applies to whitetails. Understand their body language and you'll fill more tags than ever before.

# 5

# Mapping out a Game Plan

"Show me a deer hunter who has an assortment of maps and aerial photos in his daypack and I don't even have to ask if he's consistently successful," my regular hunting partner Al Wolter once observed. "It's a given that he takes at least one nice buck every year."

Wolter is a former Deputy Director for the U.S. Forest Service, and for more than twenty years one of his responsibilities entailed managing hundreds of thousands of acres of national forest lands in several different states.

"We've always relied upon aerial photographs to give us the most accurate appraisals of the topography of any landform," Al explains. "Even though they're taken from 30,000 feet, these photos are so detailed that when studying them under a magnifying glass I can actually tell you the species of individual trees in a woodlot.

"I can remember sitting in my office studying aerial photos to compile a new forest management plan for a given region and it was often difficult to pay attention to my work," Al laughs. "I began spotting generation-worn deer trails leading to and from food plots such as mast-bearing oak trees, and this tempted me to

Hunters who study maps and aerial photos at home can learn every detail of their hunting grounds and probable deer locations.

Aerial photos are available through three agencies of the U.S. Department of Agriculture.

begin evaluating how animals were living and moving in that specific area. After that, I'd sometimes even begin daydreaming where I'd situate a stand to have the best chance at bushwhacking a nice buck."

Of course, the tremendous value of aerial photos is that they cut your scouting time a hundredfold. In just one hour of studying an aerial photo in the comfort of your den you can learn more about a five-square-mile segment of real estate than if you spent an entire week hiking the same ground. It's easy to pinpoint deer bedding areas, feeding areas, escape cover and major travel routes. Actual in-field scouting, then, need only later consist of an hour or two hiking around to confirm what you already basically know and to look for smaller and more recent sign that would be invisible in the photos—beds, tracks, pellets, rubbed saplings, scrapes and the like.

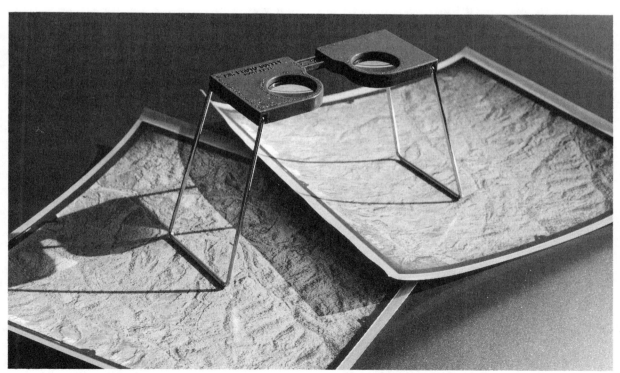

Although aerial photos can be studied with the naked eye, they are supposed to be viewed in pairs with a stereoscope.

Currently, three agencies of the U.S. Department of Agriculture rely heavily upon the precise visual information provided by aerial photos to assist in conservation practices, forest management, drainage programs, boundary determinations, watershed planning and road construction. Those three USDA agencies are the Agricultural Stabilization and Conservation Service (ASCS), the Forest Service, and the Soil Conservation Service (SCS). The combined aerial photography files they maintain presently cover about 90 percent of the nation.

Local offices of the ASCS, Forest Service and SCS generally maintain photo files only for their specific county-by-county regions. In most instances, these are black/white photos 12" x 12" in scales ranging from 1" = 4,833 feet to 1" = 200 feet, each at a cost of about $6. However, there are many other sizes available, ranging in sizes up to 38" x 38", sometimes in color. If the particular photos you're interested in are not customarily kept on file by your local USDA agency, or if they happen to be photos needed for hunting in a distant state, you can order them from the Aerial Photography Field Office, P.O. Box 30010, Salt Lake City, UT 84130.

It's important to note that although you can look at and study an aerial photo just as you would a common photo that you took yourself, aerial photos are not like one-dimensional topographic maps that we'll discuss later. Most aerial photos are intended to be viewed in stereo pairs with a handy little device known as a stereoscope. Compact stereoscopes designed for field use are available for less than $20 through companies that sell forestry supplies and equipment. One such company is Forestry Suppliers, Inc., 205 West Rankin Street, Jackson, MS 39204.

## THE STEREOSCOPE AT WORK

A stereoscope gives you a three-dimensional look at the landscape, which is absolutely critical if you want to learn about the terrain structure. It's just like watching a 3-D movie in

**A stereoscope magnifies aerial photos and creates a three-dimensional effect, as if you were flying overhead in a light plane.**

which you can see deep into valleys and river-bottoms while the higher elevations literally jump out into the forefield of view. Additionally, a stereoscope magnifies what you're looking at by 2½ to 5 times what the naked eye would see in studying the very same photo. This provides a wealth of insight because, just like fish, deer use terrain structures, and as little as a ten-foot change in elevation may have a pronounced influence upon their movements.

Most advanced deer hunters use aerial photos in two distinctly different ways. First, when striving to learn about unfamiliar terrain, they study 12" x 12" photos in stereo pairs with a stereoscope. Next, they view a much larger aerial photo of the very same tract of land.

Mine are usually 24" x 24" (they cost $12), and I mount them in a sturdy picture frame. The frame protects the photo from wear and tear but, more important, because of the glass front, I can write on the photo. Using a red grease pencil, I can mark the exact locations of physical sign discovered while scouting, property-line boundaries, where stands have been placed, or even the desired logistics in the staging of drives. This is invaluable, especially when in the company of friends who are unfamiliar with the region but nevertheless need a visual reference as to where stands are located, what routes they should take as drivers, or even how to negotiate the terrain when participating in cooperative stillhunts.

Mounting your aerial photo in a picture frame protects it from damage. You can use a grease pencil to indicate on the glass any deer sign discovered while scouting.

By studying an aerial photo you can identify the species of individual trees and determine feeding areas, travel patterns and escape routes.

## What to Look For

Of course, any given several-square-mile tract of good deer hunting habitat may reveal slight changes from one season to the next. The glass covering on my aerial photo allows me to erase last year's information and draw in the types and locations of this year's crops, where a logging operation may have been undertaken, perhaps where a forest fire ravaged the landscape, and, of course, the new scrapes, rubs and other deer sign which is sure to be evident.

To provide a striking example of the wealth of insight which can be gleaned from an aerial photo, consider just the trees themselves and how the following identification procedure can tell you what hunting tactics might be in order even months before the season opens.

Large, mature trees always appear as large dots, immature trees as small dots. If those large dots are relatively light-colored, you know in advance they are hardwoods that should be producing a varied mast crop of acorns, beechnuts, hickory nuts, or the seed-fruits of maples or poplars, to name a few. This tells you the location of a prime fall/winter food source which the animals are sure to be regularly visiting. Yet from your previous hunting experience, you also know that such mature trees create a high, overhead canopy that prevents sunlight from bathing the ground, and this means there shouldn't be much ground-level cover for midday bedding purposes or for the animals to hide in when hunting pressure begins to intensify.

Conversely, small, light-colored dots thickly saturating a tract of land represent immature

Enclose photos and maps in a plastic bag to protect them in the field. You can write on the bag itself.

saplings not yet bearing an annual mast crop. Deer may be able to browse here upon the occasional buds and branch tips that are within their reach. But for any prolonged activity they'll probably bed in the regenerative cover usually found close to stands of young trees and do their major feeding elsewhere. With your stereoscope, look for trails entering and exiting this bedding area; they will appear on the photo as thin, white lines.

On aerial photos, large dark-colored dots indicate the presence of mature conifers. Since you know that spruces, pines, firs and other evergreens constitute only starvation rations for deer when they cannot find more desirable foods, and since such species likewise shade-out brush and vegetative understory growth, it can be inferred well in advance of your scheduled hunt that these areas are not likely to be used by deer for much of anything.

However, if those dark-colored dots are small, you know it's an immature conifer plantation. Since such trees have dense whorls of branches close to the ground, they provide ideal security cover for deer, either for bedding or for escaping into when opening-day guns begin booming and hunting pressure mounts.

Moreover, if in examining your aerial photo you find trees which appear as large, light-colored dots, and if they have been systematically laid out in evenly spaced rows and tree-to-tree intervals, you've found an orchard! If the trees in question are bearing apples, peaches, or plums, they'll be a magnet to deer.

In using our orchard example, the next order of business would be to scan the perimeters of the orchard for thick concentrations of small, dark-colored dots indicating immature, dense pines the deer use for bedding cover. Later, you would hike directly to that specific edge where the security cover borders the orchard to ascertain exactly where to place your stand.

Once, several weeks before Virginia's deer season opened, Al Wolter and I, in studying an aerial photo, discovered a ten-acre clearcut in the George Washington National Forest. About three or four years after an area has been logged-off, regenerative growth affords deer splendid browsing; finding this particular clearcut would have required extensive scouting on foot. But we were able to pick out specific trees on the photo that would be likely candidates for our portable stands, even though we had never previously visited the national forest.

## USING TOPO MAPS

In conjunction with an aerial photo of your intended hunting grounds, a topographic map can add still more valuable insight because it contains much information that is not found on aerial photos.

Topo maps are compiled and distributed by the U.S. Geological Survey. They are commonly available in bookstores and through county extension agents. Or, you can write directly to the USGS, Map Distribution Center, 1200 South Eads St., Arlington, VA 22202 for maps of areas east of the Mississippi. For maps of areas west of the Mississippi, write to USGS, Federal Center, Denver, CO 80225. Since topo maps have to be ordered by quadrangle number, either office will first send you a free index listing maps available for the region you request, an order form and a price list.

By using contour lines, cartographers are able to portray land elevations in feet (generally, 20-foot intervals), thus enabling a hunter to identify ridges, valleys and the sloping or stair-stepping terrain features in between. If the individual contour lines are spaced very close together, it means the terrain is quite steep there. Wider-spaced contour lines indicate gradual changes in

the elevation, and no contour lines at all in a particular area means flat ground.

Since topo maps are multi-colored, existing cover is readily identified at a glance, but you'll have to check each map's legend to determine what the various colors represent. Blue is always water and green is always forestland. White or yellow may denote open fields, croplands or swamps.

Other features commonly represented on topo maps are the names of public roads, the names of streams and rivers winding through the terrain, and even locally familiar names such as "Wildcat Hollow" or "Buckhorn Ridge."

Finally, still another valuable item found on a topo map that is not found on an aerial photo is a distance scale, enabling you to determine how far it is from Point A to Point B (in feet, yards or even miles).

## PLAT MAPS

County plat maps are created for the purpose of assessing property taxes and are available at minimal cost from your county engineer's office, usually located in the courthouse at the county seat. Such maps show who owns every parcel of land within the county, the exact amount of acreage contained within each tract, and its exact configuration. Therefore, although a plat map probably has limited value to the hunter working several thousand acres of public land, such as a national forest, it can be an extremely important tool if the tract is smaller (50 to 500 acres) and is under private ownership.

With a plat map, you are able to size up your intended hunting grounds at a glance and familiarize yourself with prominent landmarks such as rivers, streams, county and township roads, water towers, and in some cases even buildings. This enables you to orient yourself well enough so it's difficult to get lost.

Moreover, since property boundary lines are so well delineated, there's little chance of inad-

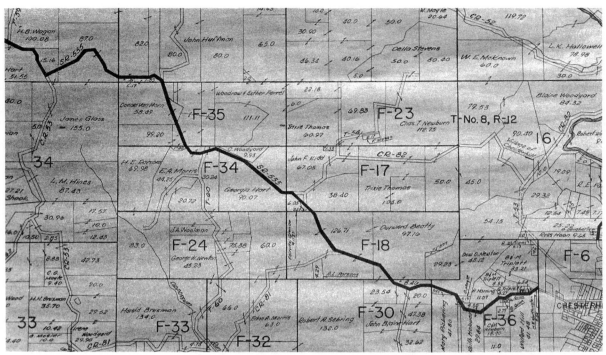

Plat maps are helpful because they show exact property lines, the
acreage of each parcel, and the name of the landowner.

vertently trespassing onto another's property and getting involved in a steamy altercation with the landowner and perhaps another party of hunters that has the exclusive use of that property. In fact, knowing the names of neighboring landowners, and how their property is laid out, can be quite helpful in securing permission to hunt upon adjoining lands or perhaps even when trailing a wounded deer that crosses a boundary line.

## SCOUT THE DEMILITARIZED ZONES

Radio-tracking studies of deer have confirmed that a surprisingly high percentage of mature bucks die of old age by learning how to avoid close encounters with hunters. Consistently taking big bucks isn't solely a matter of outsmarting the animals but also of plugging into the scouting equation the influence of hunting pressure in

a particular area. When the deer season opens, the sudden surge of human activity will disrupt the animals' otherwise normal routines and push them back into remote parts of their home ranges. This takes us briefly back to the subject of topo maps and a slick trick most experts are now using to counteract the influx of hunters.

First, use a felt marking pen containing a see-through ink to color in all the terrain lying within 1,500 feet on either side of every road and trail suitable for a vehicle. On standard 7.5-minute-series topo maps, 3/4 inch equals approximately 1,500 feet. You can now entirely eliminate this ground from any further consideration because the chances of taking a nice buck there are quite slim.

Studies of hunter pressure on deer have shown that the vast majority of hunters do not venture farther than 1,500 feet (approximately one-quarter of a mile) from some type of road or trail. As a result, these zones of hunter influ-

Few hunters venture far from where they've parked, and deer avoid these hubs of human activity.

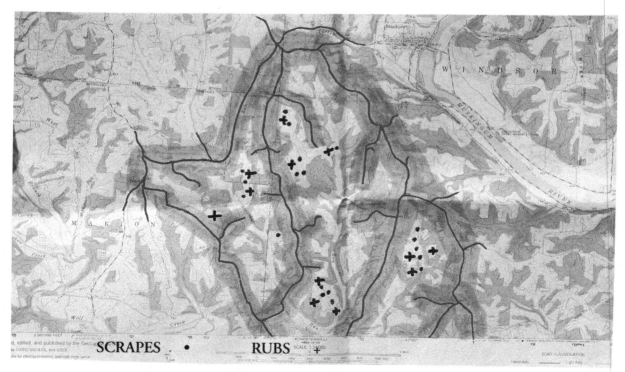

SCRAPES • RUBS +

Use a pen with see-through ink on your topo map to block out all terrain within a quarter mile of every road and trail. Then scout the interior regions. That's where you'll probably find the most deer.

ence constitute a hub of activity the deer just won't tolerate for more than a few hours.

If you are therefore working somewhat farther back in the hinterland, you'll actually double your chances of seeing deer. Not only will you encounter the resident trophy deer who prefer such undisturbed habitat in the first place, but as the days pass you should also begin seeing immigrant animals that have retreated from the 3,000-foot-wide hunter-influence zones bordering the roads.

Through the use of aerial photos, topo maps, and plat maps, you'll learn far more about your hunting grounds than you ever imagined possible. And when you know almost as much about the terrain as the deer themselves, your accumulated knowledge and insight will quickly be translated into hunting success.

# 6

## Pellets, Tracks and Beds

Considering the millions of whitetails harvested every year, it would seem that modern-day hunters are quite proficient at their sport. But actual success percentage figures released by state game departments tell us an entirely different story. The blunt truth is that most hunters are not very skilled, for in a majority of states the success ratio averages less than 20 percent. This means that this year, at best, only one out of every five hunters will be taking home a deer of *any* size, buck *or* doe.

Why is it, then, that in every camp, there are certain hunters, like my friend Tom Henderson, who seem to consistently defy the odds and take nice bucks (sometimes several of them) every year?

The answer is that once he has used a combination of aerial photos, topo maps and plat maps to become intimately familiar with the terrain to be hunted, he knows how to scout effectively and, even more important, how to analyze the sign he discovers.

"In fact, only about 10 percent of my total involvement in deer hunting is actually devoted to sitting on stand or stillhunting," Tom once remarked. "Another 10 percent is devoted to practicing with my rifle and archery equipment. And the remaining 80 percent is devoted to the study of maps and photos, and in-field scouting."

Here's another thing that is sure to startle most average hunters. Henderson is a strong proponent of post-season scouting and this means that, by the end of March, he often has already decided upon the very buck he wants to take the following fall and knows quite a bit about the animal's daily routine.

## POST-SEASON SCOUTING

Why begin in-field scouting shortly after the current hunting season has come to a close? Isn't it better to while away the winter months leisurely studying maps and photos and then reconnoiter the terrain much later, during the traditional scouting months of September and October, just before a new hunting season is about to open?

Keep in mind that when you begin scouting in January or February, the deer are still solidly locked into their fall/winter behavior modes. This means that the trails, bedding sites, and food

How do some hunters manage to consistently take nice bucks (sometimes several of them) every year? Mainly, they know how to scout and analyze the signs they find.

sources they are using can be counted upon to be used again during the forthcoming fall/winter period. As a result, you gain valuable insight that can be acquired at no other time of year.

Conversely, if you wait until September or October to begin your investigations, when many of the deer have not yet fully completed making a transition from their summer behavior patterns to their fall/winter modes, the information gained may not be entirely relevant to what will be going on when the season opens. Suddenly, the deer may almost overnight begin using different trails, bedding areas and feeding grounds, and when this happens your only alternative will be to re-scout the terrain, relocate your stands, and in so doing unnecessarily sensitize the animals to human intrusion.

Of course, winter scouting also disturbs the animals, but you needn't be concerned about occasionally spooking them and sending them running with their tails held aloft. You can even penetrate their core security regions and bedding areas—something you'd never want to do just prior to the hunting season—to learn how they are entering and leaving their chosen hiding places. Since the animals will have the entire spring and summer to recover from your intrusion, it's worth the risk of disturbing them to acquire information that will pay off handsomely later on.

## Reading Tracks

The winter period is the finest time of year to find trails and evaluate their frequency of use. With most vegetation absent and at least occasional traces of snow on the ground, a trail that may have been almost indistinguishable in October becomes strikingly obvious in January or February.

Despite the claims of many hunters to be able to distinguish between buck and doe tracks, biologists say the only conclusive method is to see the deer actually standing in the tracks.

Otherwise, it's a myth that tracks that are blunt at their tips are always a buck's and those that are pointed are a doe's. This characteristic depends upon the abrasive effects of walking in sandy or rocky terrain, not upon the sex of the animal. Whether you can see dewclaw imprints depends upon the softness of the ground or the depth of the snow.

If you carry a small tape measure while scouting, you have a better chance of telling the sex of a deer. Tracks up to 4½ inches long, measuring from tip to dewclaw, usually indicate a doe, yearling or fawn. Tracks 5 inches in length usually indicate a 2½-year-old buck. And tracks 5½ inches to 6 inches in length usually indicate a mature buck of at least 3½ years of age. Yet these are only guidelines. Like human females, some does have very big feet!

There are other clues (just that, clues!) to determining gender. Since mature bucks are usually heavier bodied than does, they often drag their feet rather than step daintily along. When a buck urinates in snow, it will appear ahead of the rear feet, while the spray of a doe will be directed backward between the rear feet.

It's also worth noting that, with the exception of the late spring and early summer bachelor buck period (to be discussed later), mature bucks are invariably solitary animals. Therefore,

It is not always possible to determine the sex of a deer by its tracks alone. But there are clues. Tracks at least 5 inches in length usually indicate a buck. Smaller tracks usually belong to a doe.

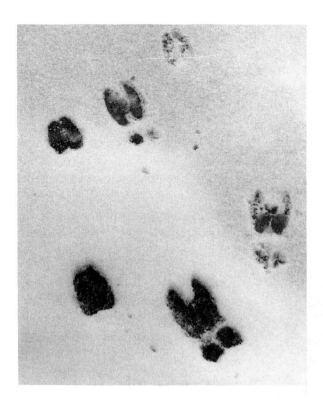

if you find a set of moderately large tracks accompanied by one or two sets of very tiny prints, it's most likely a doe with her most recent offspring.

## SCIENTIFIC SCATOLOGY

Examining individual piles of pellets is probably the most sophisticated means of evaluating how many deer are in a given region and how many of them are mature trophy bucks.

Biologists with the Wisconsin Department of Natural Resources have determined that white-tails defecate an average of thirteen times every twenty-four hours. Good deer hunting habitat will have at least twenty-five deer per square mile. This means that in every square-mile tract of land the resident animals will leave 325 piles of pellets every day! Consequently, if you do not find a lot of fresh and old droppings, you can presume there are few deer in the area.

The type of food deer eat determines the shape and consistency of their excrement. This can be valuable to the scouting effort because it

When relatively large tracks are accompanied by smaller imprints, it usually means a doe is being followed by her offspring.

A tape measure is an aid in studying deer sign. Shown here (from left to right) are buck, doe and fawn droppings.

can suggest where deer have been browsing or grazing in the immediate area. If a deer has been feeding upon grasses, forbs, or fruit, its feces are usually in the form of a loose mass of very soft pellets. When a deer has been browsing upon drier material, such as woody twigs and branch tips, the feces will be in the form of elongated pellets that are quite firm and claylike.

When discovering pellets, an advanced hunter should once again put his trusty tape measure into use and with a notepad record his findings. Generally, pellets that are $\frac{1}{2}$ inch in length indicate a doe, yearling or fawn. Pellets that are $\frac{5}{8}$ inch in length indicate a buck approaching maturity, probably a 2½-year-old. And droppings that are $\frac{3}{4}$ inch to 1¼ inches in length indicate a mature, trophy buck at least 3½ years of age.

Aside from pellet sizes, there's an even surer way to determine if deer droppings were made by a buck or doe. In most instances, doe excrement is in the form of individual, loose pellets ranging in number from 40 to sometimes more than 300. Yet buck droppings are not only individu-

A deer's diet determines the shape of its pellets. Doe droppings are generally loose and separate, like a pile of black jelly beans.

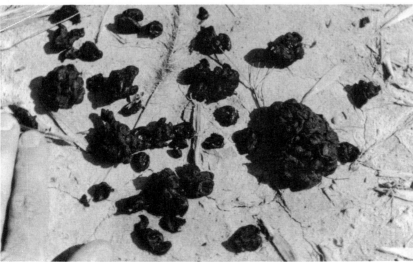

Buck pellets are quite often clumped together in large globs that may break up into smaller pieces on hitting the ground.

ally larger but are generally clumped together in walnut-size to large globs, although they sometimes break apart on impact with the ground.

## FINDING THE BEDS

Most hunters cannot resist the temptation to follow deer tracks, to see where the animal is going. But I like to do the reverse. Rather than follow the deer, I follow his tracks in the opposite direction to learn where he has been, in the hope of finding his bedding region.

A key piece of information that ties all of this together is that, while whitetails may defecate almost anytime or anywhere, the vast majority of whitetail defecation occurs shortly after the animals rise from their beds. Moreover, the quantity of pellets on the edge of the bed indicates the length of time that a deer remained in that particular spot.

This is valuable insight when it comes to deciding upon a strategic stand location. Perennial advice given to deer hunters is to situate a stand somewhere between the deers' feeding and bedding areas in order to ambush them as they go back and forth. Well, ascertaining feeding areas is not difficult, especially in farm country, but finding bedding areas can be a brow-furrowing exercise in frustration. This is because mature bucks rarely bed in exactly the same spot each day. Rather, they have bedding areas, seldom leaving a pronounced matted oval that is easily detected unless snow or damp leaves are present.

When you do chance upon a bed here or there, take the time to measure it. Beds that are 40 inches or less in length usually indicate a doe, yearling or fawn. Beds 45 inches in length usually indicate a 2½-year-old buck. And beds 50 to 56 inches in length usually indicate mature bucks 3½ years of age or older.

Study how the beds relate to each other. Several small beds accompanied by one large bed usually indicate a doe with her current off-

Search for lone beds that are at least 50 inches in length as they are almost always those of mature bucks.

**Finding beds is essential to success because they indicate core security areas where mature bucks spend up to 90 percent of their time.**

spring. Several clustered beds of somewhat larger size usually mean several mature, same-age does. And a lone bed is frequently that of a mature buck.

In dry weather, when there is an absence of readily visible beds, many individual piles of old and fresh pellets in a relatively small area saturated with dense cover is a sure indication of a bedding area. Closer examination of the pellets should next offer clues as to the sexes of the animals. But there is yet another way in which this discovery is helpful.

Within the home range of each whitetail there is an approximate 40-acre "core area" where the animal spends up to 90 percent of its time. This core area offers the best combination of desirable attributes to be found within the animal's much larger home range. There will be easy access to water and a prime food source, to

be sure, but of even more concern to deer, especially mature bucks, the core area will be virtually free of human disturbance. In short, a core area offers a buck a greater sense of safety than anywhere else within his home range.

As a result, when hunting pressure begins to mount and the biggest bucks in a given region become almost exclusively nocturnal in their feeding, drinking and other activities, you know exactly where they'll be sequestered during the daylight hours. They'll be hunkered down in their beds, somewhere in their core areas! And because you've already determined the location of these bedding regions by finding and analyzing tracks and droppings, staging an effective drive (which I'll describe later) could be the answer.

If you prefer to stillhunt in solo fashion, however, which I'll also later describe in detail, keep in mind that a characteristic of whitetails when

**Deer usually bed facing downwind, with their legs splayed to the left. Knowing this, a hunter stands a good chance of sneaking up on a bedded buck.**

they are bedding is that they usually lie with their legs splayed to their left and face downwind. Therefore, if the wind is from the south, for example, a careful stalk from the east, moving toward the bedded deer's back or blind side, would be more likely to succeed than a stalk from the south, in which case the buck could easily smell you, or from the north or west, in which case he'd be likely to see your approach.

## OTHER SCOUTING CONSIDERATIONS

On several occasions we've described measuring pellets, tracks and beds, but at this point a word

of clarification is in order. The measurements I've presented here should not be looked upon as universal because across the country there are thirty different subspecies of whitetails, many of which have body sizes and other anatomical features that differ somewhat from their cousins living elsewhere.

The figures presented here represent the Northern Woodland deer *(Odocoileus virginianus borealis)* which is found throughout the upper Midwest and east into New England. This is our largest whitetail and, consequently, its tracks, pellets and beds are typically larger than other subspecies that inhabit the Deep South and Southwest.

I mention this because a hunter will want to take pellet, track and bed measurements at every opportunity, keep records of his finds and then compare them to other sign found in the same vicinity. Thus, in short order, he should be able to measure pellets or other sign and instantly know whether that sign represents a mature buck in his particular region or a smaller buck or doe.

By now, the reader may have noticed that we haven't had much to say about the trails deer customarily use on a day to day basis. I prefer to save most of that information for our later discussion of tree stands and ground blinds.

In post-season scouting, there is one other form of sign to be on the lookout for: shed antlers, which are readily visible during the months of February and March. When you find a shed, you can infer that particular buck managed to survive the previous hunting season and that this is his home range. You know the size of his previous year's rack and can therefore make an educated guess as to what his headgear will look like the following season. And you can equate the antlers with associated tracks and other sign to dope out that specific animal's behavior patterns.

Likely as not, although he'll soon go into spring and then summer behavior modes, possi-

Search for shed antlers because they represent bucks that have survived the hunting season and still are in the area. Since antler characteristics are generally the same from one season to the next, you'll also know what his rack will look like next fall.

bly in a different location, he'll be right back doing whatever allowed him to survive the previous hunting season. What better way to learn the whereabouts and lifestyle of a whopper buck so you can begin making plans to collect him next year.

Shed antlers can be found almost anywhere, but there are certain places where they are found with greater frequency than elsewhere. First, check fencelines, especially where there are low spots where deer jump to cross over. The impact of their front hooves striking the ground frequently causes a loose antler to be jarred free. Since deer spend a greater amount of time bedded during the winter period than any other time of year, in order to conserve energy in the face of sharply reduced food supplies, known bedding regions are also splendid locations to find shed antlers.

"It's both challenging and rewarding to pursue deer hunting in such a manner that a buck never knows he's being hunted and that he never realizes his behavior, in large part, was doped out almost a year in advance," my friend Tom Henderson asserts. "But perhaps the biggest thrill comes after your deer is down and you can compare his present antlers with his former sheds from the previous year. If they show a distinct similarity, you know almost with full certainty that it's the same buck you pre-scouted last winter, and that is something that gives any advanced hunter immense pride and satisfaction."

# 7

## Find the Food, Find the Deer

Wildlife biologists claim it is far easier to make a list of foods deer will not eat than those they do. One study several years ago revealed 614 different varieties of plant life in North America that whitetails consume at one time or another. In fact, aside from the breeding season, the remainder of the year sees deer so inextricably tied to their known food sources it's almost axiomatic that if you find their local favorites you'll find the deer themselves nearby.

Interestingly, however, whitetails anywhere don't generally spend a tremendous amount of time feeding, as the act requires the use of sensory and thought-process energies that otherwise might better be invested in keeping tabs on whatever is going on around them. In other words, when deer are actively feeding, you might say they have one-track minds, and this makes them vulnerable.

Therefore, nature has made ruminants of the members of the deer family, which means that they possess stomachs containing four compartments, enabling them to feed rapidly and with only minimal amounts of chewing and swallowing. The food ingested goes first into an upper

stomach known as the rumen, where it is temporarily stored. Later, after the deer has retired to a safe resting place, from which it can monitor its environment, it regurgitates the partially chewed food to complete the job. When the "cud" is well masticated and then swallowed a second time, it enters the next compartment of the stomach, known as the reticulum, and from there travels to the omasum, through the abomasum, and then into the intestines for the remainder of the digestive process.

## KNOW YOUR HUNTING GROUNDS

Those are the basics. But from here on, any discussion of whitetail feeding habits becomes somewhat complicated and may require a good deal of individual interpretation.

Certain types of forage occur in one area but not in another. There are annual fluctuations that may produce a boom in mast crops and other foods, and scant supplies the following year. Also, the maturity dates of certain foods vary, so the deer have to switch to the most

When deer are feeding they are oblivious to what's going on around them. So nature has made them ruminants with four-compartment stomachs to allow them to feed quickly.

After feeding, deer retreat to bedding locations where they can monitor their bailiwicks and chew their cuds.

Latitude has a great influence upon the feeding activities of deer. In the Far North, starvation rations are often the rule.

tender, palatable and nutritious forage at specific times.

There also are latitudinal influences: deer in warm climes have ample foods year-round while their cousins farther north may be "yarded" in winter in confined quarters and deep snow that restricts their movements and forces them to exist on starvation rations.

So the important thing is your evaluation and interpretation of the area you will be hunting. One of the best ways to begin is by consulting someone who is well acquainted with the study of trees, vegetation, plant life and crop species. This is most likely to be an agronomist or botanist affiliated with the U.S. Forest Service or an agricultural extension agency.

Whoever you make contact with, show him

the list of preferred deer foods presented below and ask which ones are prevalent in your region, and in what kinds of soil or terrain they usually grow, so that you can locate them when you're scouting.

Nationwide, of the 614 native foods deer are known to eat (which may include at different times of year the buds, flowers, leaves, shoots, branchlets, berries, or nuts of those trees or plants), their distinct favorites are *red maple, aspen, pinion pine, witch hazel, poplar, huajilla, staghorn sumac, mountain maple, arbutus, honeysuckle, horseweed, white cedar, juniper, dogwood, white oak, osage orange, greenbrier, wintergreen, hemlock, ash, willow, crabapple.*

The domestic foods deer relish more than any other include *Imperial Whitetail Clover, soy-*

*beans, alfalfa, red clover, white clover, ryegrass, winter oats, cabbage, blackberry, elderberry, lettuce, corn, apples, lespedeza, trefoil, carrots, blueberry, cranberry, sugarbeets.*

Of course, most deer hunters can identify common foods such as acorns. But how many of us can readily identify horseweed, witch hazel or staghorn sumac, among others, which deer will revisit every day if it is available? (Incidentally, staghorn sumac, which is easily recognized by its twisted, disfigured branches and bright red seed clusters, is especially favored by deer during bitter-cold winter months because the plant is exceptionally high in fat content and when digested helps deer generate body heat.)

Moreover, when it comes to oak trees, proper identification is essential because deer prefer the acorns of some oak species over others. To illustrate how complicated this can be, here's a list of different oak species: northern red oak, scarlet oak, shumard oak, pin oak, black oak, southern red oak, nuttal oak, blackjack oak, water oak, laurel oak, willow oak, live oak, white oak, swamp white oak, chestnut oak, bur oak, swamp chestnut oak, post oak, chinkapin oak and overcup oak. We've just mentioned twenty different species of acorn-bearing trees, some of which deer consider to be ice-cream foods while others are rarely touched, and I've listed only those particular oaks found east of the Mississippi.

Consequently, in addition to talking with a local agronomist or botanist, I strongly suggest you obtain a pocket-size manual of trees and plants, with color identification pictures, for ready reference in the field.

In evaluating suspected feeding sites, keep in mind that other critters may be utilizing the same food source, and you don't want to mistake their signs of feeding for those of deer. Three examples are worth noting. When you find small fragments of acorn shells, they're probably the work of squirrels, not deer; deer usually crush the shells longitudinally into large halves or thirds. When you find ears of corn

Since many other animals share the whitetail's range and utilize the same food sources, learn to recognize signs of their feeding. Only the very tip of this corn cob has been bitten off, indicating a raccoon at work, not a deer.

with just the tender tip bitten off, they're the work of raccoons, not deer; deer nibble randomly upon the entire ear. And when you find low vegetation sheared off cleanly, it's the work of rabbits; deer have a rough-textured "grinding pad" in their mouths and plants on which they've fed have a ragged and torn appearance.

## GROW YOUR OWN TROPHY BUCKS

"When deer are forced to get by with whatever nature provides, they are continually in a survival-mode," deer biologist Larry Weishuhn explains. "But when hunters and landowners enter the picture and begin providing deer with

**Biologist Larry Weishuhn: "Nature alone does not provide deer with enough sustenance to consistently produce racks like this. But with supplemental feeding by hunters and landowners, they can grow trophy racks."**

plenty of extras, trophy bucks are the result. Consequently, deer hunters who have their own property, lease lands, or have access to private land, are putting in highly specialized food plots for deer and other wildlife."

Is there any particular domestic food that deer universally favor over all others? According to test results by the Whitetail Institute of North America, the vegetation preferred most by deer is a new type of ladino clover blend known, coincidentally enough, as Imperial Whitetail Brand.

According to the institute, which serves as a central clearinghouse of research information devoted exclusively to the whitetail deer, this newly developed clover blend is certain to revo-

lutionize the sport of deer hunting because it improves the overall quality of the species and greatly enhances antler growth.

I thought about that remark as I looked down upon a small food plot from a nearby tree stand. Below me were four does and two bucks, and whenever they periodically turned at just the right angle to the early-morning sunlight, their coats glistened like neon signs. Even more impressive, both bucks sported larger antlers than we customarily see in southeastern Ohio.

"The reason the deer appeared to shine was because of lanolin in their coats," Weishuhn explained, "and this, along with the larger than average antlers, was due to an abundance of body mineral the deer couldn't have obtained from native forage alone."

To satisfy their nutritional needs, whitetails require about seven pounds of bulk food per day. Yet the big mistake made by hunters and landowners is providing this sustenance only in the spring and summer when deer need help the least. Instead, they should be setting the table for deer during the worst of times.

This is critically important because nutritional intake goes first to meet basic survival needs of an individual deer. It is only after these requirements are met that excess nutrients are channeled into fawn development, antler growth and resistance to diseases. Now you know why, some years, does in a given region have only single fawns and most of the bucks have thin, spindly antlers. The previous winter was particularly hard on them and their body metabolisms commandeered virtually all spring and summer nutrient intake just to return them to a state of normal health. Consequently, when a given region is not producing large numbers of deer, and few quality bucks, it is almost always because nutritional foods are available there only on a seasonal basis.

"This is exactly why I got involved in the development of Imperial Whitetail Brand Clover," says Ray Scott, director of WINA "It's an exciting deer food that will make the dreams of hunters come true wherever it is planted. That's because most quality grass forages such as alfalfa and others offer only 16 percent protein content, but the clover blend we designed offers an average of 25 to 30 percent protein!"

Even more significant—and this goes back to our earlier mention of the importance of deer receiving highly nutritional food on a year-round basis—Imperial Whitetail Clover does not turn woody and stemmy in late summer and does not brown-out and go dormant in winter like other grass forages. Rather, it remains green, tender and succulent twelve months a year throughout the U.S. and Canada. Moreover, it adapts to a wide

Imperial Whitetail Clover remains green, lush and palatable year-round, even in northern climates. It attracts deer from surrounding areas.

Ray Scott, president of the Whitetail Institute of North America: "The new ladino clover blend we developed has a 25 percent protein content compared to other legumes that are only 16 percent, and this translates into improved growth rates and antler size."

range of soil conditions and does not require annual reseeding.

"As for palatability, deer prefer Imperial Whitetail Brand Clover 5 to 1 over cattle-type grasses," says Scott. "On our research grounds, the clover literally sucks deer out of surrounding regions. They walk right past other foods they'd otherwise stop to nibble upon to reach it."

What is even more astounding than Imperial Whitetail Brand Clover's ability to draw deer from afar is the effect it has upon antler growth. On the Whitetail Institute of North America's research grounds, where deer had the opportunity to dine upon this unique clover blend over a brief period of only four years, spike bucks entirely disappeared! Every eighteen-month-old

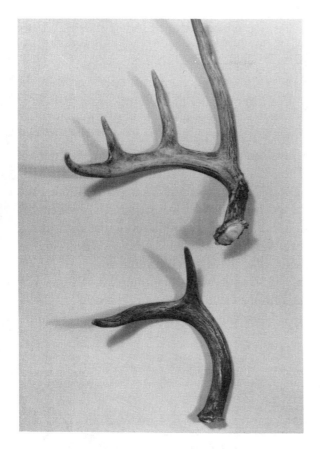

**Dramatic proof of the effect of Imperial White-tail Clover on antler growth. These are the first year's antlers produced by two bucks. The lower antler was from a deer that foraged on native foods. Top antler came from a buck that had subsisted primarily on new clover blend.**

buck sporting his first antlers had a six-point rack or better!

The reason for these incredible results is easy to explain. When deer are well fed year-round, they do not have to undergo a spring recovery period. There's no required bounce-back time to compensate for winter's toll. And this means that when spring arrives, does may immediately get on with the business of birthing and nursing healthy twins and triplets, and bucks may immediately begin laying down a foundation for heavy antler growth.

Imperial Whitetail Brand Clover is not expensive, and this makes it an ideal planting project for individuals or hunting clubs. If you cannot find it at a local seed supply dealer, write to the Whitetail Institute of North America, Route 1, Pintlala, AL 36043, or call 1-800-688-3030.

## Other Food-Plot Choices

"Although a high-protein diet is essential for healthy deer and the production of big antlers, other considerations also enter the picture," biologist Larry Weishuhn asserts. "Hunters who possess their own land, or have leased lands, or have close relationships with farmers should maintain diversified food-plot plantings to offer their deer a smorgasbord of good eating.

"I recommend hunters establish two types of food plots," says Weishuhn. "One should consist of winter foods to help animals through a period of great physiological stress. Ideal foods to plant include oats, winter wheat, triticale or Austrian winter peas. Corn is also a great food because of its high carbohydrate content. But since this requires heavy-duty farm equipment to plant, it's faster and less expensive to buy several rows of corn from a large field a farmer has planted and tell him to leave it standing.

"Late spring and early summer food plots are also necessary," Weishuhn continues, "because during this period deer require ample nutrition. Does must give birth to healthy twins, nurse them and then wean them onto nutritional solid foods. Meanwhile, bucks are experiencing the critical developmental stages of antler growth. In these food plots, I recommend hunters plant sorghum, hilgari, alfalfa, soybeans or summer peas."

## Easy Planting Techniques

Many hunters shy away from the prospect of planting nutritious foods to help their deer, so it's important to point out that establishing several food plots does not require much acreage, equipment or hard work, and the financial investment is small compared to other routine hunting expenses.

Take, for example, the small amount of hunting land I own in southeastern Ohio. Not long ago I put in an Imperial Whitetail Brand Clover food plot for year-round foraging by deer, a spring/summer food plot of alfalfa, and a winter food plot of oats. My total cash outlay came to less than $100 for seed and fertilizer. The time involved in preparing the three sites and planting the seeds amounted to roughly twelve hours. And the equipment was no more sophisticated than the rototiller and assorted hand tools used in my vegetable garden every year.

Since deer are creatures that like to keep on the move while eating, food plots should be small and widely spaced. Instead of undertaking the arduous task of putting in a single one-acre food plot somewhere, much better would be to put in three smaller plots, none larger than, say, fifty by fifty feet, and each in a different location. Strive to make these food plots easily accessible to deer by situating them in small clearings in forestland cover rather than in wide-open fields or hillsides. This accomplishes two things. First, it will encourage and allow deer to utilize the food during all hours of the day; otherwise, they'll be inclined to visit the food only at night. Second, as a direct result of the first, during hunting season you can stillhunt or sit on stand in the vicinity of your food plots.

As to actual planting techniques, establishing

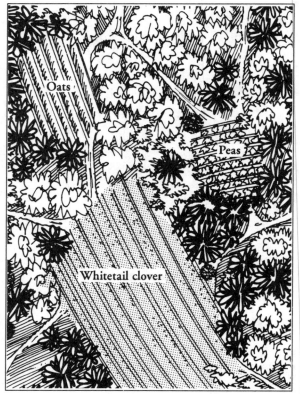

**Instead of planting one large food plot in an open area, it is much better to plant several smaller plots with different food choices in or near heavy cover to encourage deer to feed during the day.**

A hunter doesn't need heavy farm machinery to establish food plots. A common garden tiller is sufficient.

Seeds can be evenly dispersed with a shoulder-bag spreader, or you can simply broadcast them by hand.

food plots is not difficult, especially with grain seeds that tend to be quite small and do not need to be covered with more than a half inch of soil. As noted above, I use my garden tiller to rough up the surface of the ground. The seeds can then be sowed by broadcasting (throwing small handfuls) or by using a shoulder-bag seeder for a more even distribution. Then go over the ground again with the backside of a rake to cover the seeds and, finally, broadcast handfuls of fertilizer such as 12-12-12 or triple-13.

## Government Seed Packets

Because establishing food plots has proven to be so beneficial to all wildlife species, many state game departments are now offering so-called wildlife seed packets to the public. These two-pound seed packets are usually free, the only requirement being that you must own or lease a minimum of five acres of land. If you don't own or lease land, you can obtain the same seed packets from your local Soil Conservation Service office for a very nominal price and then plant the seeds (with permission) on the private land where you hunt.

The contents of these packets may vary between states in accordance with different climatic and soil conditions, but they all contain a wide assortment of seeds which will germinate into plants favored by deer and other wildlife. The most recent packets I obtained and planted contained seeds which later produced very diverse food plots containing sunflowers, millet, corn, orchard grass, rye, soybeans, birdsfeet trefoil, red clover, oats, black-

State wildlife departments commonly offer free wildlife seed packets to hunters and landowners. Since a dozen or more different plant species are in each bag, a cornucopia of good eats awaits deer and other wildlife.

Mineral supplements in block form enable deer to lay down heavy antler growth in early spring and summer.

Mineral supplements are also available in granulated form. Select a brand that is high in sodium, zinc and manganese.

This young buck almost seems proud of his very first rack, which could not have been achieved without the benefit of supplementary food and minerals.

berries and probably some other plant varieties I couldn't identify.

## Mineral Supplements

Numerous studies have shown that mineral supplements in excess of what is naturally available in any habitat will produce dramatic results in antler size and herd reproduction. These supplements are available in block and granulated form, but a hunter may be at a loss as to which of the many available brands are best.

"In conjunction with my research into the nutritional needs of deer, I had friends from throughout the whitetail's range send me freshly shed antlers," Larry Weishuhn recently told me. "We then took core samples from these antlers and analyzed them for their primary composition."

What Weishuhn discovered was that the bigger antlers were much higher in sodium, zinc and manganese than other antlers. So good advice is to read the ingredients labels on any mineral supplement you're considering, to learn which particular brands are highest in the above elements.

Although mineral supplements are marginally expensive, especially if you buy them in 25-pound block form and have them mailed to you, they go a long way. You need only one so-called "mineral lick" for every 40 acres of deer habitat and under normal conditions should have to replace it only once every two years.

One word of advice, however. In some states, hunting over a mineral block may be illegal. It's usually a waste of time, anyway, because bucks visit the blocks most frequently in spring and summer when their antlers are in the developmental stage and they need a lot of minerals. In the fall and winter, this need does not exist and they visit mineral licks infrequently.

# 8

# Antler Rubs Tell All

When I first saw the buck from a distance, he was loping down an acorn-littered oak ridge, and I was convinced that, after twenty years of pursuing deer, I was about to be awarded a chance at a very high-scoring Pope & Young whitetail.

The deer appeared to have a ten-point rack, but what was especially impressive was its spread, which I estimated to be at least twenty-five inches. I slowly raised my bow and waited.

I rank what happened just a few minutes later among my most bizarre deer hunting experiences. The deer closed the distance to within thirty yards when I suddenly realized it was not a record-book buck at all, but merely an average 2½-year-old eight-pointer. The supposedly big rack I had seen from a distance wasn't entirely comprised of antler material, but included a mutilated sapling which had become wedged between the animal's main beams and rearmost bay tines.

The buck had apparently so ravaged the sapling during the rubbing episode that he had completely uprooted the young tree and carried it off. Thoroughly disappointed, yet equally amazed, I lowered my bow, raised my camera to record the event, and then had a good laugh. A photo of that deer appears here.

Then I began thinking about the rubbing behavior of bucks and how it constitutes part of a complex method of communication between deer.

Of course, whitetail mating behavior has long fascinated hunters and biologists alike, and many myths have circulated among hunting camps for generations. We still do not fully understand every aspect of rubbing behavior, and even among the most respected scientists there is occasional disagreement. Nevertheless, every year new information surfaces. The astute hunter who keeps abreast of these findings is sure to refine his knowledge of whitetails, and it is this educational process which translates directly into more and bigger bucks hanging on the meatpole.

First, to dispel a few old wives' tales, antler rubs do not indicate places where bucks have removed their velvet and then polished and sharpened their tines. When a whitetail's maximum annual antler growth has been attained,

From a distance I thought this was a record-book deer, until he came closer and I saw an uprooted sapling wedged in his antlers.

Forget the myth that bucks rub their antlers on tree trunks to remove the velvet. In truth, the velvet dries and falls away of its own accord.

Beneath the antler velvet, a buck's rack already is smooth and the tines are sharply pointed, with no need for the buck to hone and polish them.

The diameter of a rubbed tree is important. As a rule, mature bucks rub both large- and small-diameter trees, but immature bucks rarely rub large trees. A rub of this size indicates a very large buck is in the area.

the skinlike velvet dies, dries and begins falling away in shreds, mostly of its own accord; the entire shedding process is often completed in less than eight hours. About the only time a buck hastens its removal is when an annoying, stringy remnant hangs down and blocks his vision, whereupon he briefly thrashes his antlers on a nearby shrub.

In any event, once the underlying antlers are fully exposed, the main beams are already smooth, and the tips of the tines are pointed. There is no need for the buck to hone them like a gladiator readying his swords for battle.

The height of the rub is also of no importance and does not indicate the size of the buck that made it. But the diameter of the rubbed tree is indeed significant. Large trees indicate large bucks, and small trees represent the work of young ones. But here again, you must be careful and not to search only for large rubs. The rule of thumb is that big bucks sometimes rub small trees as well as large trees, yet it is very rare for small bucks to rub large trees.

What, then, is the buck's purpose in rubbing trees? He wants to leave numerous calling cards, in the form of olfactory signposts, to alert as many does as possible to his presence. But he also rubs a certain number of unusually large-diameter trees to create visual signposts, in order to warn other mature males that this is his breeding territory.

As to the exact significance of individual antler rubs, most biologists believe that they serve the purpose of enabling each buck to establish a breeding territory of sorts. It should be emphasized that whitetails are not territorial in the true sense of the word, as it would be quite impossible for even a dominant buck to drive all other male deer out of his home range. As a result, in most regions, several or perhaps many bucks must share the same turf.

Still, despite the fact that whitetails are not territorial, they must nevertheless acquire a breeding area where they feel secure, while simultaneously obtaining a social status which gives them breeding privileges over subordinate or lower-ranked animals.

## FIND THE EARLY RUBS

There are two distinct periods when a majority of antler rubs are created. The first rubbing activity usually occurs during the first three

The purpose of rubs is to serve as visual and olfactory signposts that communicate with other bucks and does. Note the distinct "rub line" here where numerous trees have been whacked as this buck proclaimed his breeding area.

weeks of September, when bucks are still in their bachelor groupings. Now is when they are developing their herd rankings. This is when they decide, within their local society, which are the superior animals and which are the subordinates. Moreover, the very first rubs are made by the dominant bucks in the region, due to their anxiety to get on with the business of firmly establishing the herd pecking order.

How many rubs does a mature buck make? According to deer biologist Larry Marchington, a mature buck makes anywhere from 69 to 538 rubs in any given year, or an average of 300 rubs. With the peak rubbing period of mature males being the first three weeks in September, this means a dominant buck can be expected to make at least 14 rubs a day.

Hunters should therefore mark on their aerial photos or topo maps the exact locations of the first rubs they discover during early scouting missions, as they were likely made by the largest deer in the immediate area. Confirmation of this suspicion, of course, comes in the form of noting the sizes of the rubs; they should be at least 2½ inches or larger in diameter.

The second flurry of rubbing activity takes place during the first week of October. This is when the other, lesser deer in the region engage in their rubbing.

Another revealing thing we've learned about whitetails is that a buck's antler-rubbing behavior is directly tied to seasonal mast production. When there is a bountiful mast crop, a hunter can expect to find a much higher number of rubs than usual. Conversely, in years when mast production is low, rub densities may be 30 to 60 percent less than that of the previous year! That's because a buck's physical health is dependent upon mast. Acorns, in particular, but other types of mast as well, are transition foods that deer utilize shortly after hard frosts kill the lush vegetation they've been feeding upon during spring and summer but before they've fully switched to browsing upon twigs and branch tips. As a result, when there is a poor or virtually nonexistent mast crop, the mid-fall physical condition of the animals deteriorates just enough to reduce the vigor and intensity with which they engage in pre-rut rubbing.

Keep this in mind when you are scouting, and if you are not finding as many rubs as you'd expect, don't automatically conclude there are few bucks around. Take the time to check a number of oak ridges or hardwood forests to evaluate the mast crop. If you find very little mast, bucks are most likely in the area, but they are simply rubbing less that year. On the other hand, if mast is plentiful, but rubs seem markedly absent, chances are the buck population is indeed quite low.

Interestingly enough, biologists now have reason to believe that the peak of the rut may change slightly from year to year as a result of the bucks' activity and their ability to influence the does' estrous cycles.

Essentially, what happens is this: When there are a greater number of buck rubs in a given area than normal, it's quite likely that an earlier than usual estrus will take place among local does because of so-called "priming pheromones"

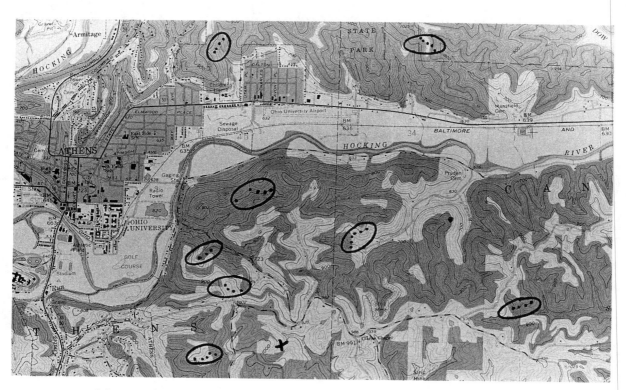

Mature, dominant bucks are the first to engage in rubbing behavior each fall. On a topo map or aerial photo, mark the location of the earliest antler rubs to appear and you'll have a good fix on the whereabouts of the biggest deer in the area.

**Annual mast production plays a role in rubbing behavior. If mast production is low that year, there may still be plenty of bucks around, but their rubbing has simply been retarded.**

deposited by bucks rubbing their forehead glands on trees. These scents secreted by bucks, when deposited in greater quantity than usual, have been found to induce early ovulation in does, pushing the peak of the rut forward.

The priming pheromones that induce early ovulation in does also have the effect of suppressing the already lower testosterone levels in young bucks, thereby effectively reducing their aggressiveness and competition for breeding privileges.

In nature's mysterious way, this well-planned scheme is designed to benefit the herd. Young bucks, which are chemically induced into a low position in the breeding hierarchy, engage in minimum reproductive effort and experience less late-season weight loss. They are thus better able to make it through the upcoming harsh winter months and are more likely to grow larger and healthier the following year when they are destined to become dominant breeding animals themselves.

## SCOUTING YOUR BUCK

When a buck leaves his bedding area, heading in the direction of a known food source or mak-

After a buck creates an antler rub, it may then rub its forehead glands on the exposed cambium to deposit priming pheromones.

Priming pheromones induce early ovulation in does and push the peak of the rut forward. They also chemically suppress testosterone levels in immature bucks so that dominant males will have less competition for breeding privileges.

In scouting for antler rubs, check pockets of aromatic tree species such as conifers, dogwood, sassafras. Bucks prefer such species because their resinous cambiums hold deposited scent much longer.

ing his rounds to check scrapes, he occasionally rubs saplings adjacent to the trail. In time, distinct "rub lines" are created. Savvy hunters can interpret these signs and, with a high level of accuracy, ascertain the direction the animal was traveling and even the time of day he made the rub. With this information at hand, being in the right place at the right time becomes infinitely easier.

But first, you must have a general idea where to begin conducting your search for rubbed trees. Again according to biologist Marchington and his research, 26 percent of all rubs are found along deer trails, 10 percent along old logging trails, and 15 percent along stream banks in valleys. The remaining 49 percent are random rubs created along field edges, woodlot clearings, in the vicinity of thickets, and throughout forested regions. Investigate such places, especially where there are pockets of ter-

rain known to have aromatic trees, such as cedars, pines, spruces, shining sumac, cherry, dogwood and sassafras. In the absence of these species, bucks will create rubs on virtually any species, but they distinctly like the ones listed above. The most commonly accepted explanation for this preference is that the oily, resinous cambiums of these species will retain the buck's forehead gland scent longer. In the case of nonaromatic species, scent deposited by rubbing might conceivably wash off during the next rainstorm, thereby making the rub less effective as an olfactory signpost.

As mentioned earlier, I suggest hunters mark on a topo map or aerial photo the locations of each rub they find, *especially* the season's first rubs which are indicative of the largest bucks in the region. If this isn't done, each discovery may seem totally happenstance. But when you can study large numbers of individual rubs on a map, your perspective broadens, and often a pattern can be discerned that reveals distinct rub lines and thereby the trails a buck is using.

With this accomplished, it's time for a closer investigation of the individual rubs comprising the overall rub line.

If the tree is rubbed on the downhill side, you can bet that it was made in the morning when the buck was ascending to his midday bedding area; hence, you've found a trail worth watching during the *morning* hours. Conversely, if the rub is on the uphill side of the tree, the deer was probably coming downhill in the evening to feed or search for ready does in the lower elevations; this trail calls for an evening stand.

A similar situation takes place in flatland terrain, with rubs found in open feeding areas and around the perimeters of woodlots generally having been made during the night hours and rubs deep in heavy cover generally having been made during midday.

During the course of his scouting, a hunter often chances upon an area of intense rubbing activity where it seems virtually every tree within fifty square yards has been ravaged. The hunter's first thought is that a monster buck vented his pent-up sexual frustration in the area. In reality, the hunter most probably found a rub concentration which is not overly significant, at least in terms of pegging the whereabouts of a mature buck.

Rub concentrations are created early in the season when bucks are still in their bachelor groups. If there are two or three bucks keeping company, and they are all of the same age-class and carrying antlers of roughly equivalent size, chances are that they're having difficulty establishing their hierarchal roles and determining who's who on the totem pole. This is especially true among immature $1\frac{1}{2}$- or $2\frac{1}{2}$-year-old bucks.

As a means of intimidation, one of the bucks is likely to rub a sapling while the other two watch. Another buck is then likely to respond

This rub reveals a great deal about the buck that made it. The diameter of the tree indicates the rub was the work of a big buck. The degree of mutilation says the animal was in a very aggressive mood. And since the rub faces away from deep cover, it undoubtedly was made in early morning as the deer was traveling from an open feeding area to his bed.

by saying, in effect, "Oh yeah, well watch this!" Whereupon he demonstrates his prowess by rubbing another tree. The third buck then responds by putting on his own show. This rubbing activity can go on for an hour or more, and when the animals finally depart, it looks as though not a single tree has been left untouched.

Although the appearance of a rub concentration can be quite awe inspiring, it probably will not prove to be a good hunting location when the season opens. By then the bachelor groups will have long since disseminated, abandoned their late-summer/early-fall travel patterns, and adopted their own individual breeding territories elsewhere.

## POST-SEASON SCOUTING TELLS ALL

As described in Chapter 6, one of the best times to study whitetail behavior is in late winter and early spring. The exposed cambiums of rubbed trees will not have weathered yet, and trails will be easily discernible. Moreover, like the game "connect the dots," an astute hunter can often spot consecutive rubs leading off into the distance, and by drawing imaginary lines between them can determine that particular buck's precise travel pattern.

According to whitetail expert Dick Idol of Bigfork, Montana, make note of those trails with not only large-diameter trees that have been rubbed but those with at least one rub for every twenty feet of trail, for this is undoubtedly the travel route of the region's largest dominant buck.

Additionally, keep in mind that mature bucks very frequently rub the same trees from one year to the next. If you examine a fresh rub, you'll probably detect weathered scarring which has healed over from the previous season. Be absolutely sure to note the locations of these particular trees, because if the buck that created them survived the just-concluded hunting season, he's almost sure to rub them again next year.

By following a rub line and its associated trail, you can also ascertain the bedding area the buck is using. This is vitally important, because you will not want to situate your stand too close to the bedding area.

Aside from rubs serving as olfactory signposts that influence the estrous cycles of local does, their second and equally important function, as noted earlier, is to serve as visual cues among local bucks. In effect, an antler rub is an extension, as it were, of a given animal in that deer's absence, and it serves to communicate information to other bucks which may filter through that same region at a later time. That means that no matter where you're hunting, there's a great likelihood that at least several bucks are sharing the same bailiwick and even using the same trails.

When a buck comes ambling down a trail littered with rubs, you should know instantly whether the deer is just a so-so deer or the dominant buck in the immediate region. If it's a subordinate deer, seeing the large-diameter rubs

**Expert hunter Dick Idol of Bigfork, Montana: "Find a trail where there is a large-diameter rubbed tree for every twenty linear feet and you've found the travel route of the region's biggest buck."**

In addition to serving as scent-posts, a buck's antler rubs serve as visual cues, proclaiming this as his breeding area and for all other males to stay away.

along the trail will cause him to adopt a submissive body posture, a slinking gait that reminds me of a retreating dog that has just been swatted on the rump with a newspaper for wetting the floor. The tail is held tightly against the hindquarters, the back is somewhat sunken, and the head is held low.

If a buck exhibits this behavior, you can take him or not, depending upon what fulfills your expectations for concluding a successful hunt. But realize the deer's body language reveals that he is intimidated by the rubs in the area and that the trail is also being used by a much larger animal.

A dominant buck behaves differently. He'll hold his head high and may actually have a somewhat prancing gait, almost like a high-stepping quarterhorse. But the sure tip-off is that he will periodically lift his tail to half-mast and extend it straight back for long moments at a time. If you observe this behavior, you might as well go ahead and take the deer at the first opportunity, because, in that particular region, he's at the very top of the social hierarchy. The only other alternative, if you are hoping for a still larger buck, is to pull your stand and spend your remaining hunting time elsewhere.

Learn to decipher the fascinating language of antler rubs and you'll have a greater appreciation for the complex social lives of whitetails. More important, your success in taking big bucks will dramatically increase.

# 9

# Analyzing the Rut

The beginning of the rut is something you can sense. It is a collage of unseasonably crisp air temperatures, woodsmoke curling from fireplace chimneys, wind rustling through still-standing cornstalks, jack-o-lanterns, and sex-crazed bucks that bound across highways at night and are briefly illuminated in the paths of automobile headlights.

Probably for as long as man has hunted, the cosmic forces that control the onset of the rut have been shrouded in myth and fable. For generations, hunters have maintained that polar air masses sweeping down from the north have been responsible for changing the body metabolism of whitetails and arousing their sexual inclinations. But this theory has never been able to account for the rutting phenomenon in the Deep South, where even mid-winter days may be quite warm. When we lived in Florida, I used to scrape-hunt in 80-degree heat and frequently saw deer copulating.

In truth, it is not air temperature that triggers the so-called rut. It's a post-autumnal equinox phenomenon known as photoperiodism. When the days begin growing noticeably shorter, a doe's behavior is changed by the decreasing amounts of daily sunlight passing through her eyes. This results in a type of electrical, reverse-stimulation effect upon the pituitary gland. It causes its normal function of regulating body growth to cease temporarily while simultaneously spurring increases in the secretion of progesterone (the female sex hormone) to bring does to a heightened state of readiness. (As mentioned in the previous chapter, bucks are able to accelerate a doe's readiness by depositing priming pheromones on the exposed cambiums of trees they've raked with their antlers.)

So herein lies another myth of sorts, for whitetail bucks do not really go into rut, as has been demonstrated in several revealing studies. In the most significant, a doe and buck were placed in a large fenced compound. At various times of the year, the doe was injected with progesterone to artificially induce a state of estrus, whereupon the buck instantly was all over her. It did not matter whether the month was March, June, or December; once he got a whiff of the good stuff, there was no denying him his pleasures.

**Contrary to popular belief, bucks do not go into rut. They are eager to breed for many months. Only when the females go into their estrous cycles does breeding occur.**

However, as revolutionary as these findings are, they bear a note of qualification. Although a whitetail buck is like an ordinary male dog in that he will attempt to mount any female that's in heat no matter what the month, he is capable of actually impregnating her only when his antlers are hard and velvet free. It is only during this time, a period spanning the months of September through March, that his elevated testosterone level produces a healthy, motile sperm count.

Nevertheless, in the world of whitetails, it's actually the does that go into the so-called rut. Their brief annual periods of sexual readiness, during which they discharge characteristic odors and fluids, tell bucks they are now willing to submit to their advances.

## WHEN THE RUT BEGINS

Exactly when this sexual activity can be expected to peak each year, and consequently when scrape hunting is the most exciting, is unquestionably one of the most hotly contested issues in deer camps nationwide. But two scientific studies, both very similar in nature, seem to have drawn the greatest acceptance among hunters and scientists alike, and they are worth briefly recounting here.

From 1961 to 1968, New York State biologists Lawrence Jackson and William Hesselton studied the embryos of 864 dog- and road-killed does of various ages. Since the average whitetail gestation period from the time of conception to the time of birthing is 202 days, Jackson and Hesselton were first able to determine the ages of the embryos and then, by back dating, to pinpoint the exact dates each of the 864 does was impregnated. After plugging still other variables into their rutting equation, the scientists were then able to create a graph portraying a core model of the rut for whitetail deer living anywhere in the United States.

What I've recounted here is merely a distillation of the lengthy and quite elaborate procedures that were employed. But what's especially noteworthy is that Jackson and Hesselton ascertained the date of November 15 as being the peak of the whitetail doe rut nationwide.

In the accompanying graph, reproduced from their research, the November 15th breeding peak is quite apparent. But notice as well that a classic bell-shaped curve encompasses the dates of October 10 through December 31 before breeding activity begins to taper off sharply. The reason for this is that does, like humans, are individualistic, and although there is a common period in which a majority of animals peak in their sexual activity, many others begin coming into estrus as much as a month earlier or later than the others. In fact, yearling does often are impregnated at only eighteen months of age, yet this first-ever estrous cycle they experience is generally about thirty days later than that of mature does 2½ years or older.

What I find especially intriguing, however, is that although this study points out the importance of hunters keeping November 15 in mind, perhaps of even greater importance is October 31. For several weeks prior to this date, the female sex hormone progesterone begins to seep into the doe's system; but it is approxi-

**By determining the age of deer embryos, biologists can tell when a given doe conceived and thus date the peak of the rut in that particular region.**

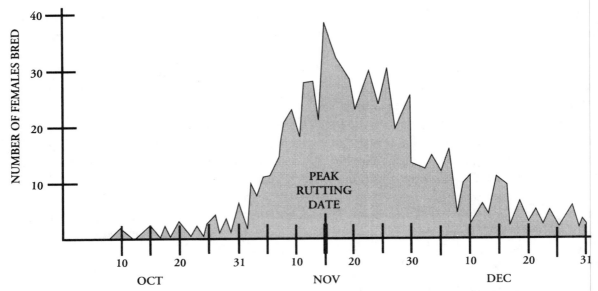

This graph, produced by the author's research of the Jackson-Hesselton study, depicts rutting intensity. Note the November 15 peak, but also the mid-December activity when does that aren't bred earlier come back into estrus a second time.

Rutting activity starts out slowly at first but then suddenly explodes, causing bucks to tend scrapes and tirelessly chase does.

mately on Halloween, for some strange reason, that a large percentage of does begin rapidly climbing to their sexual peaks. Then each day sees it more and more difficult for any given buck to cover all bases.

In the same graph, note as well the slight resurgence in breeding activity in mid-December. This undoubtedly accounts for a certain percentage of does coming into estrus a second time twenty-eight days later after failing, for one reason or another, to conceive during their first heat.

## MORE STUDIES AID HUNTERS

A second study by Robert D. McDowell ("Photoperiodism Among Breeding Eastern Whitetailed Deer," 1970) took basically the same procedural approach but was much more elaborate in scope. McDowell recruited the help of deer biologists in nineteen states throughout the whitetail's native range to analyze the ages of embryos taken from 4,663 does. He then cre-

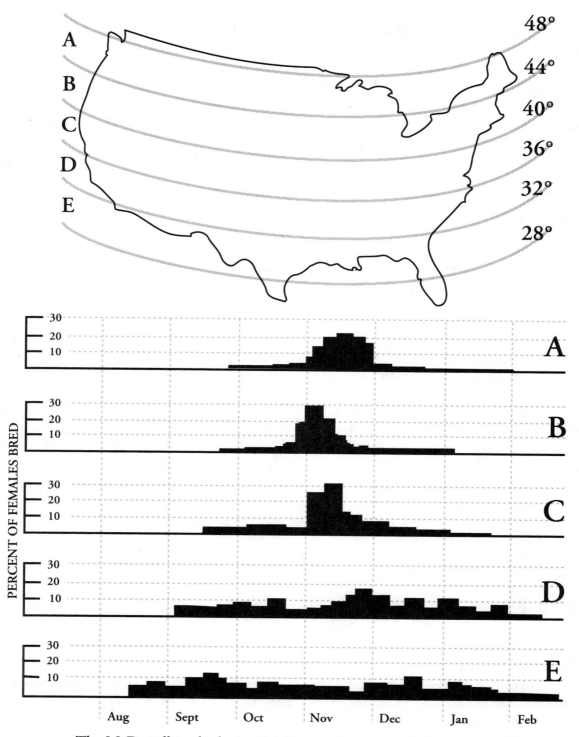

The McDowell study depicts rutting activity in accordance with latitudinal influences. Note the well-defined rutting activity in the northern states, but the less-intense rutting activity in the South that is drawn out over many months.

ated a bar graph depicting the breeding-date peaks in five geographic regions.

North of the Mason-Dixon Line, McDowell's peak breeding period closely conforms to the earlier findings of Jackson and Hesselton. But notice that the farther south one ventures, peak breeding times become far more erratic.

To date, many theories have been expounded to explain these oddities. One speculation has to do with soil fertility levels as they relate to deer habitat. Many states in the southerly latitudes have large tracts of spartan habitat ranging from desolate swampland in the easternmost and southernmost regions which gradually yield to desertland as one enters Texas and continues westward. And in such areas where available forage is of low nutritional value, deer that are forced to survive on deficient diets breed later than deer on high-nutrient diets elsewhere (such as the farm belt of the upper Midwest).

Similarly, according to biologists Larry Marchington and David Hirth in their book *Whitetailed Deer, Ecology and Management* (Wildlife Management Institute, 1984), in northern states local variations in the breeding season seem to be minimal, but in many southern areas significant variations occur within a single state.

For example, in Florida, Mississippi and south Texas, the onset of the rut and the occurrence of actual breeding vary by as much as two months at distances of only 100 miles. In fact, in those regions where seasonal conditions show little variation, such as southern Florida, some degree of breeding occurs during all months of the year!

Still other exceptions to the rule come to mind. Georgia, for example, is the only southern state, to my knowledge, which has a well-defined peak rutting period. It occurs during mid- to late November, owing to the unique subspecies of whitetails living there.

Decades ago, Georgia's whitetail population was severely depleted and restocking was accomplished by transplanting live-trapped whitetails from Wisconsin. Wisconsin's peak of the rut is mid-November, and many succeeding generations of those transplants still are "cycled" in accordance with their ancestral lineage. Perhaps, in decades to come, the transplanted subspecies will become entirely "southernized" and exhibit breeding activity much later; in neighboring Alabama, which has not seen an introduction of deer from a northern state, the majority of breeding activity takes place in January.

In summary, then, throughout the whitetail's northernmost range, annual breeding activity is an intense, frenetic period in which so-called scrape hunting is charged with almost explosive levels of excitement. In northern Michigan, this activity may peak on November 5. In Ohio, as we've noted, it generally peaks November 15. Then there are other states, such as Illinois, which spans a distance of over 350 miles from its northern border with Wisconsin to its southern tip adjacent to Kentucky and Missouri. There the peak of the rut in southernmost Pulaski County may occur as much as two full weeks later than in northernmost Winnebago County. And as one travels still deeper into the southernmost ranges of whitetails, mating can be described as a rather mild-mannered activity that extends over a span of many months.

Since there are so many exceptions to these rules, I strongly suggest obtaining a wall map titled "White-tailed Deer Populations" from Scientific Hunters Division/Information Outfitters, 1995 Daniel Lane, Yulee, FL 32097 (phone 904-277-4046). This colorful map was compiled by the Southeastern Cooperative Wildlife Disease Group from data gathered from all state wildlife agencies. Not only does it reveal deer-density populations on a county-by-county basis nationwide but also contains a handy reference chart showing peak rutting dates for every state (or various areas within states where the dates may vary).

Interestingly enough, game managers of state

wildlife agencies north of the Mason-Dixon Line, through no intentional malice, have actually taken steps to prevent some of us from hunting the rut. A game manager's first responsibility is to manage game, with recreational hunting given only second priority. And one page in the game manager's handbook stresses the goal of maintaining maximum numbers of each species, consistent with what the available habitat can support. Accomplishing this necessitates taking measures that ensure the animals can achieve their maximum reproductive potential.

Consequently, if you've ever wondered why most gun-hunting seasons north of the Mason-Dixon Line do not open until mid- to late November, you now have the answer. By then, the peak of the rut has passed, a majority of the does have been successfully impregnated, and now hunters may begin harvesting bucks with the assurance that come next fall, deer populations will still be at the same high level. Conversely, throughout the South, gun-hunting seasons open as early as late August in some states, and often extend well into January. There simply is not much in the way of a peak rutting period upon which to base hunting seasons or restrict the annual harvest of deer. Also coming into account is the fact that deer populations per square mile are significantly higher in the southern states than farther north, and yet hunting pressure is less—two factors that justify more lengthy gun-hunting seasons.

A hunter who lives north of the Mason-Dixon Line and who has been reading between the lines should intuitively know that if he is to reap the greatest enjoyment from rut hunting, it is imperative that he take up bowhunting, for this is the only allowable way to pursue rutting whitetails. In fact, in one survey of bowhunters that asked what initially attracted them to the sport, a good percentage said that using primitive equipment presented a greater challenge and each success in taking a deer was therefore more rewarding. However, a great many hunters noted as well that they were attracted to bowhunting because they could take advantage of the rut and have the best possible chance of downing a whopper buck.

Not surprisingly, the same attitude toward bowhunting does not prevail in the southerly latitudes. There are high numbers of Dixie bowhunters throughout the South, to be sure, but gun hunting is undeniably more popular, for the simple reason that one does not have to master specialized equipment to enjoy hunting the rutting period.

## FIND THE DOES, FIND THE BUCKS

As essential as it is for early-season hunters in the northern states to resort to the stick-and-string, employing the right strategies is equally important.

For example, when our Ohio bowhunting season opens on October 5, scrape-hunting is not yet a worthwhile endeavor. Bucks are just beginning to scrape and it seems to be a rather half-hearted affair at best, with virtually all scrapes seeing only sporadic revisitation. Therefore, the best opening-day strategy in Ohio and other northern states is trail watching. This may sound like ancient advice, but it has nothing to do with distinguishing between buck tracks and doe tracks in order to watch a buck trail. Actually, that's the last thing you want to do!

During the spring and summer months, bucks form bachelor groups and do indeed cling to their own trails and establish travel patterns often quite different from does. And if deer hunting were permitted at this time of year, watching a buck trail could indeed be counted on to produce action.

However, several weeks before Halloween, when a region's first does begin coming into heat and leaving splashes of estrous urine along their travel routes, groups of bachelor bucks begin breaking up, and the males fall into hierarchal

Throughout the summer, bucks remain in bachelor groups and use their own trails to segregated feeding areas.

ranks based on their ages and aggressiveness. Moreover, their travel tendencies undergo a change as well. They exhibit behavior known as "transference" and begin to use doe trails. This stands to reason, because once a buck gets a snoot full of estrous urine, he focuses on just one thing—catching up with the particular doe in the vicinity that is just beginning to enter heat.

For the next couple of weeks, bucks also engage in what is known as "tending," which involves constantly maintaining close contact with a doe that is steadily progressing in her climb to sexual readiness, patiently waiting for just the right moment when she will permit herself to be bred.

Doe trails, then, are the ones to find while you're scouting, and being able to distinguish between buck and doe tracks is crucially important. As mentioned in Chapter 6, a lot of bally-hoo has been written about this subject, but we as hunters can at least make educated guesses.

The vital clues I rely on most often are smaller sets of imprints accompanying a set of much larger tracks. This is a good indication that a doe is being followed by her offspring of the current year. As her estrous period begins to heighten, she'll invariably chase away her young, but at least for the time being they'll still be with her, as will other offspring following their own mothers. Bingo! You've found a doe trail. Next, find a place where two or three such trails either cross or converge to form a main runway, and you're close to identifying an ideal stand site.

But don't become too complacent with these initial efforts, because as more and more of a given region's doe population approaches its estrous peak, the time for scrape-hunting, the subject of the next chapter, will arrive.

## DON'T MISS THE RUT REPLAY

As mentioned earlier, does frequently experience follow-up estrous cycles. This can be partly attributed to nature's intended design that all creatures reproduce. Yet, due to a variety of complicated biological reasons, many does that are bred by bucks do not successfully conceive. As a result, it is nature's decree that these animals have estrous cycles every twenty-eight days to increase their chances of reproducing into the spring months.

Mankind is also partly responsible for whitetails having more than one mating period. According to the laws of nature, harmony in the animal world means a balanced sex ratio of one female for every male. Yet for many generations, mankind upset this balance by protecting does and harvesting bucks only.

It has been only in recent years that biologists have recognized the need for harvesting does as well as bucks. Yet many regions of the country have been slow to recover, and this often is clearly evident in a sharp sex-ratio imbalance of sometimes as many as twenty-five does to every buck. This makes it very difficult for a given buck to find and breed with every doe in his region. Consequently, in portions of many states, does may experience recurring estrous cycles as many as five times until as late as March, whereupon a buck's

**To find out if there's a second rut in your region, check former scrapes to see if they have been reopened and freshened with renewed scent deposits. Or ask a local biologist about the doe-to-buck sex ratio of the deer in your area.**

Since most fawns are born in early to mid-spring, a sure indication of recurring rutting periods is seeing late-born fawns in midsummer.

testosterone level diminishes and he is no longer capable of impregnating a doe (even though he may copulate with her). These recurring estrous cycles in does in effect cause additional "ruts" to take place, with all the ramifications of the first, primary rut, except on a progressively less intense scale.

There are two ways to determine if subsequent rutting periods are taking place in your particular locale. First, ask a biologist about the sex-ratio of your deer population; if there is a doe-to-buck ratio of at least 5 to 1, you can be relatively sure at least one follow-up rut is taking place 28 days after the initial mating period. If there is a ratio of 10 to 1, or greater, there

may be several follow-up rutting periods.

Also, keep an eye peeled for fawns beyond the usual early-spring birthing period. If, in mid- to late summer, you occasionally see fawns that are quite small and still have their cream-colored spots, you can assume they were born later than usual, indicating their mothers didn't conceive until they had one or more follow-up estrous cycles.

Hunting secondary rutting periods can be accomplished by first finding doe trails. But you may also wish to hunt over former primary scrapes that bucks will have reopened. Finding and identifying primary scrapes is treated in the next chapter.

# 10

# Scraping up a Buck

For most serious hunters, the peak of the rut, no matter what the date in a particular region, is the highlight of the deer season. And no wonder, because deer hunting authorities have long said the only weak chink in a trophy buck's armor is a brief period of time when his hormones are racing out of control, compelling him to return to his scrapes time and again in the hope of seducing estrous does.

"Some trophy bucks are so well educated and wary they are simply unkillable," my friend Jackie Bushman once noted. "The exception is the peak of the rut when they are inclined to do some goofy things. That's about the only time you might catch one of them being a little careless."

Scrapes, of course, are the catalysts that serve to unite male and female deer. They are generally circular-shaped places on the ground where a buck has pawed away the sod, vegetation and fallen leaves to bare mineral soil. And because biologists have ascertained that whitetails make at least five different types of scrapes—each with its own significance and level of importance in the social order to which deer rigidly adhere—understanding which specific scrapes

should be eliminated from consideration and which others should be diligently hunted can go a long way toward helping a hunter consistently hang up nice bucks.

## ESTROUS-RESPONSE SCRAPES

An estrous-response scrape is the least likely to produce a buck sighting. When a doe approaches the onset of heat, chemical changes in her endocrine system are discharged whenever she urinates. If a buck happens to come upon one of these scent deposits, he'll instinctively make a scrape right there on top of the urine-dampened earth.

Estrous-response scrapes are easily identified for what they are because they seldom exceed eight inches in diameter and are never found near a mutilated, overhanging tree branch. Most of them are found around the perimeters of fields and meadows where deer have been feeding at night, or in doe bedding regions, but they can be found almost anywhere else as well. If you periodically check back, you'll find these scrapes are not freshened.

An estrous-response scrape is not worth hunting. It is a happenstance where a buck detected the urine from a doe in heat.

Of course, there's always a slight chance that you might take a buck in the vicinity of an estrous-response scrape. It should be emphasized, however, that a hunter's success in such an instance is usually the result of watching a general travel corridor that is occasionally used by deer. Otherwise, the scrape itself is merely a happenstance.

## BOUNDARY SCRAPES

Boundary scrapes are a bit more complicated to describe, and they may or may not be productively hunted, depending upon several related circumstances. Boundary scrapes have all the usual scrape features, except one. They are of average size, they are located beneath tree branches which have been broken and chewed upon, but they seldom seem as fresh and steaming hot as other scrapes. This is because boundary scrapes are laid down around the outermost perimeter of a buck's home range, and they are therefore visited less frequently than other scrapes where the buck spends most of his time. Because these particular scrapes randomly dot the periphery of the buck's territory, knowing how to recognize typical home-range boundaries of deer will in turn help you to identify such scrapes.

Although it sometimes seems as though whitetail bucks are inclined to go anywhere they damn well please, radio-tracking studies have shown that they actually spend as much as 90 percent of their time in about a 40-acre "core area," in which they have the best combination of food, water and security cover at their immediate disposal. Furthermore, when they do periodically leave the safety of their core areas to venture into surrounding or outlying regions, they are reluctant to go beyond major man-made or natural barriers (assuming, of course, that they are not being chased by dogs or being subjected to intense hunting pressure). Because these obstacles tend to restrict the bucks' travels, the obstacles, in large part, serve to establish the irregularly shaped home ranges (usually no more than two square miles in size) in which the bucks are destined to live out their entire lives.

Just a few examples of home-range boundaries, or barriers, include superhighways (especially if

Boundary scrapes dot the periphery of a buck's home range and are likely to be found along edges where woodlots yield to open ground and at the edges of natural obstacles such as lakeshores and canyon rims.

they are bordered by high fences), wide river courses, lakeshores, sheer rock bluffs, steep mountain ridges, canyon rims, and even those particular forest edges that yield to wide expanses of prairie or open ground. There is a great likelihood that scrapes found along any of these types of well-defined edges are boundary scrapes.

Deciding whether or not to hunt boundary scrapes hinges upon your assessment of the local doe population. If there is a high doe-to-buck ratio, I wouldn't hunt boundary scrapes; a buck has all the female companionship he can handle within the inner sanctuary of his home range, and there's simply no need for him to go looking elsewhere.

Conversely, if doe numbers are low, boundary scrapes may reveal regular buck sightings. Bucks now need to travel far and wide in order to service the available does, and this means regularly patrolling not only their core area but also the periphery of their home range.

## SECONDARY SCRAPES

At this point it is important to mention that all buck scrapes except one (the estrous-response scrape) begin life as secondary scrapes. It is not until many weeks later that a small percentage of these secondaries will become elevated in status to either primary or community scrapes. Therefore, early in the season—until early November in the northern states and until about mid-December in the southern states—all scrape-hunting will be done in the vicinity of secondary scrapes. There simply are no primaries in evidence at this time.

Studies have shown that a mature buck 2½ years of age or older will make an average of twenty to thirty-five scrapes throughout his home range. As noted, some of these will be outlying boundary scrapes that are seldom revisited except when there are few does in the vicinity. Consequently, the secondary scrapes you'll want to begin hunting early in the season will

Studies have shown that a mature buck makes twenty to thirty-five scrapes in his home range, but all of them begin life as secondary scrapes.

be those located within the buck's core area.

Ascertaining buck core areas is a relatively easy matter that simply involves wearing down a good deal of boot leather. Watch for an abundance of concentrated sign in the form of tracks, beds, droppings, rubbed saplings and scrapes themselves. You should find some tracks, beds and droppings that are very old, some that are moderately old, and some that are fresh. This is the best indicator of almost continuous presence of the buck in his core area over long periods of time.

In reconnoitering the terrain and deciding where to build a blind or install a portable tree stand overlooking secondary scrapes, I would strongly caution against hunting too close to the deer's bedding area. To a buck, his bedding area is the single most important place within his

core area because it's where he feels safest during the daylight hours. If a hunter gets too close, the deer may move to a new bedding area.

If I were hunting secondary scrapes early in the season, I'd want to be in a buck's core area, in a tree stand at least 200 yards from his bedding area. Moreover, that tree stand would be on the downwind side off one of the many trails filtering to and from the bedding area and upon which at least one secondary scrape is to be found. With this setup, I could slip into my stand and wait for the buck to make an appearance as he returns to his bedding site in the early morning or as he leaves in the late afternoon.

Hunting secondary scrapes early in the season is basically a hit-or-miss proposition in that all

Finding buck core areas entails plenty of scouting. Look for a combination of both old and new sign, which indicates a buck's presence over long periods of time.

of the scrapes in the core area are of relatively equal value. In other words, the buck in question does not specifically favor one scrape over another, and his revisitation is random. About the only way to tip the odds slightly in your favor is by hunting those particular scrapes located on heavily used travel corridors leading from bedding areas to feeding grounds. Or hunt what are known as "scrape concentrates." These are places where you find numerous scrapes in a relatively small or confined area. For example, if you find a tiny half-acre clearing in a huge, wooded tract, and six or seven scrapes peppered around the perimeter of the clearing, you've found a scrape concentrate.

## PRIMARY SCRAPES

In coming weeks, a small percentage of secondary scrapes seem to become magically transformed into primary scrapes and begin warranting each buck's special consideration and attention. Yet few hunters realize that it's the local does which perform this function, not the resident bucks. How all this happens involves an intriguing bit of biology.

First, understand that whitetail bucks are not at all territorial; many bucks commonly share the same home range and, in many cases, even have overlapping core areas. As a result, the many secondary scrapes littering the woodlands in a several-square-mile region may be the products of perhaps a dozen bucks or more. These scrapes serve to inform the local does that these bucks are around, but more important, the does can smell the scrapes and determine the current state of health of the individual bucks in residence.

That's right—it is the doe that decides which particular sire she wants to breed with. A doe instinctively knows that the successful propaga-

It's the doe who determines which buck she will breed with by sniffing the scent in his scrape. This unusually large scrape was made by a dominant, virile male.

tion of her species depends upon her successful impregnation by a virile, healthy male, and nature has given her a way to determine this. In smelling a buck's urine in one of his secondary scrapes, a doe is able to recognize certain chemical byproducts. Virile, healthy, mature bucks metabolize fats and carbohydrates, and they release the byproducts of this in much greater concentrations than do equally healthy but immature bucks. Furthermore, bucks that are old, beginning to degenerate in health, and are beyond their reproductive peaks, metabolize proteins, and this is equally evident in their urine.

In effect, then, each doe may investigate a number of scrapes made by different bucks before deciding which buck she wants for her sire and where she will allow the mating to take place. She then urinates in that appropriate scrape, depositing her own unique glandular secretions and remains in the general area, waiting for the buck to return.

Upon making his rounds and randomly checking his secondary scrapes, the buck will suddenly come upon the doe-scented scrape, recognize it for what it is, and elevate this scrape immediately to primary-scrape status. The buck then proceeds to scent-trail the doe until he eventually catches up with her, establishes a "tending bond" until the precise moment that she gives the "go" signal, and then copulates with her in short order.

This apparently well-ordered plan quickly turns into pandemonium as the rutting period intensifies toward its peak, because not every doe experiences her estrous cycle at precisely the same time. Furthermore, in any given region, there may be upward of fifty or more males and females, all healthy and capable of reproducing.

**On checking his scrape and finding estrous doe scent left in his absence, a buck puts his nose to the ground and quickly begins scent-trailing her.**

**When a buck catches up with a near-estrous doe, he establishes a "tending bond" until she reaches the peak of her cycle and submits to his advances.**

As a result, a buck may conclude the impregnation of one doe and immediately take up the trail of another and then still another as he continually checks and rechecks his few primary scrapes.

Correctly identifying primary scrapes is not difficult because they seem to be in a perpetual "muddied" state as they are repeatedly cleaned of windblown debris and freshened with new urine deposits. Conversely, the recently abandoned secondary scrapes will quickly become hard and dried out, and partially covered with drifting leaves and other forest duff.

From this point on, areas around primary scrapes are the places to hunt, at least until the rutting period is over and the deer return to their former activities.

Primary scrapes are easily identified because they are repeatedly cleaned, manicured and anointed with fresh scent.

## COMMUNITY SCRAPES

Still another type of scrape created by whitetails is perhaps the most fascinating of all. It is known as a community scrape and it consists of a primary scrape that is simultaneously used by several bucks that share overlapping core areas within their home ranges. Generally, the bucks in question are of the same age, have nearly equivalent racks and therefore all rank about the same in the local pecking order. Because there is no rigid hierarchy distinguishing the animals, a given scrape does not become the personal property of one buck or another, and it therefore enjoys revisitation by different bucks, each hoping to eventually discover a doe's estrous urine. While there, the buck will clean the scrape, hook at the overhead branch with his antlers and leave his own scent.

Consequently, if a hunter stays well attuned to the scraping activity in the region he's hunting, various members of his hunting party may all take nice bucks near the very same scrape over a period of several days. The initial requirement is that someone must first take a buck near a scrape. Then, each day someone must return to that very location to examine the scrape. If it isn't freshened within two or three days, it can be presumed the scrape was a former boundary scrape, secondary scrape or primary scrape made by the animal now hanging on the camp meatpole. If there are signs the scrape has been visited and freshened, you know for sure it's a community scrape. Get another hunter on that stand, pronto! There's an excellent chance he'll soon have a shot at yet another buck in the area.

## MOCK-SCRAPING

The great difficulty in hunting scrapes is that quite often they are so situated that a hunter has to settle for a stand not really to his liking. Advanced hunters now resort to "mock-scraping." The hunter, not the buck, determines where scrape-visitation is to take place. In accomplishing this, a hunter can literally pick up a scrape and move it to the location of his choice so that the wind is always in his favor and an ideal tree is available for a stand.

There are many variations and nuances to mock-scraping, so I'll describe the method that works best for most hunters.

The first order of business is to find a hot primary scrape that already is being revisited. Assuming you cannot hunt that specific spot because of any number of reasons, scout the immediate vicinity for another place that would be ideal for a hunting setup. Try to make sure the new place is within 150 yards of where the primary scrape is located and that there is not

**A hunter can move a scrape to a more desirable stand location! Note rubber boots and gloves to prevent contaminating the scrape with human scent.**

only a suitable tree for your stand but also another, nearby tree with an overhanging branch no more than six feet off the ground and beneath which you can place the scrape.

The next task is actually moving the scrape. For this you'll need a clean plastic pail, a small trowel, pruning shears and several feet of thin wire, all of which should be made entirely scent-free by dousing them with boiling water. From this point on, handle the equipment only while wearing rubber gloves to avoid contaminating them with your human scent.

At the new scrape location, construct a scrape beneath the overhanging branch by using the trowel to scuff away fallen leaves, sod, weeds and other matter down to bare mineral soil. Make the scrape about 18 to 20 inches in diameter.

Now, return to the original scrape location and, again using the trowel, shovel the top one-inch layer of muddied, urine- and scent-soaked soil into your pail. After that, use your pruning shears to remove the chewed, mutilated, scent-marked overhanging tree branch. This is a key step because it will destroy that specific primary

scrape location and prevent further revisitation.

At the new location, sprinkle the pail of scented soil over the top of the newly created scrape. Then, wire the scent-marked branch to the existing overhead branch. Both of these procedures ensure that the buck will instantly recognize his familiar scent deposits, which will lend great authenticity to the substitute scrape and therefore promote a rapid transferral of the buck's attention to the new location.

Now for the icing on the cake, to enhance the effectiveness of your scrape relocation.

To fully inveigle a buck into believing other does are visiting the bogus scrape, you'll want to anoint the scrape with a commercial scent such as doe-in-heat scent or a combination of doe-estrous and tarsal gland secretions.

However, instead of merely sprinkling the scent on the phony scrape, so that inclement weather could quickly obliterate it, I recommend using a scent-dispensing system designed for the purpose. There are several variations on the market, but they all consist of some type of scent-holding bottle or other container that can be tied

When moving a scrape, remember to cut off the scented overhead branch and wire it in place at the mock-scrape location. A buck will recognize his scent and adopt the new scrape.

to a tree branch directly above the scrape, and a drip regulator to permit fresh concentrated scent to fall into the scrape a drop at a time.

The particular scent dispensing system I'm currently using is called the Drip-U-Lator, made by Flow-Rite (107 Allen St, Bruceton, TN 38317). It contains five fluid ounces of Dominance Plus Rut Lure, formulated from stabilized doe urine and 100 percent wild whitetail tarsal glands. When hung upside-down and put into operation, it will deposit the attractant 24 hours a day, in hot or cold weather, for 14 to 21 days.

There is still quite a lot we do not know about whitetail mating behavior, and this chapter has touched upon only small slivers of what is certainly a much larger pie. But I'm convinced that in the future both conventional and mock-scraping methods will prove to be among the most revolutionary and widely practiced deer hunting techniques.

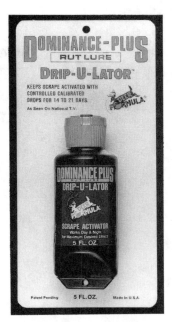

A mock-scrape scent dispensing system such as this deposits doe urine a drop at a time for up to twenty-one days, ensuring that the mock scrape attracts and holds a buck's attention.

# 11

## Rattle-in Your Buck

A cache of venison might last a year, but memories of the hunt last a lifetime. And over the years, the cumulative influence of memories shape the deer hunter's personality. In effect, an advanced hunter actually becomes a product of his past adventures, and this ties the knot of his marriage to deer hunting all the more secure. No longer is "deer hunting" simply a week-long vacation from regular routine; it is a year-round love affair that has become part of his very fiber.

I became an advanced deer hunter in the fall of 1974. I had hunted whitetails for many years before that, but this was the year my dedication to the sport became sharply elevated. Sitting in a bowhunting stand one morning, I was going to attempt to rattle-in a buck by banging antlers together in a mock simulation of two male deer dueling with each other.

What had gotten me all fired up was a magazine article by the venerable Byron Dalrymple in which he described using the technique with good success on his ranch in Texas. In a later telephone conversation with Byron, he said rattling had become the rage in his part of the world. But he said that, owing to the explosive

behavior of rattled-up bucks, he didn't recommend this technique for those with weak hearts.

As I smacked the two antlers together, I thought perhaps Byron had slightly exaggerated the excitement he claimed rattling generated. But moments later, loud crashing noises in the brushy ravine below sent my blood pressure surging, and seconds later I saw an eight-point buck charging in my direction!

The deer came only within fifty yards of my stand and then slammed to a halt as abruptly as if it had run into an invisible wall. Then it began craning its head to one side and then the other, searching. The buck was sure he had heard two other males fighting near one of his scrapes, and now he seemed angry that he couldn't find them.

During the course of the next several minutes, the deer traveled in a 180-degree arc around my stand area, intensely looking for the supposed intruders and occasionally stamping his feet, flaring his nostrils and erecting the dark tufts of hair surrounding his tarsal glands. He was mad alright and ready for battle, yet just as frustrated as if he'd been denied the pleasures of a doe.

In responding to the distant sound of antlers clashing, bucks often rush in with antlers lowered expecting an aggressive encounter with other male deer.

Then, apparently satisfied that any other males in the area had heard his approach and run off, the buck began slowly walking away. Now it was I who became frustrated. Here was the first buck I'd ever attempted to rattle-in—a real dandy—and he was gradually fading away into the brushy ravine.

When the buck was almost entirely out of sight, I figured I might as well gamble. It was a slim chance, but I picked up the antlers anyway and barely clicked the tines together just once. Instantly, the buck turned and came stampeding right back up the hill like a mad dog, his rack held low to the ground as he charged ahead in a blind rage. Everything happened so fast that I didn't have a chance to reach for my bow. Then, some mysterious sixth sense must have alarmed the buck, for he threw his tail aloft and evaporated like a wisp of woodsmoke.

It was after the deer was completely out of sight that I finally noticed my hands were trembling and there was a weak, rubbery feeling in my legs. Byron Dalrymple was right.

However, there is an important postscript to this anecdote. This experience did not take place in Texas, where rattling was born and has long been heralded, but in Pennsylvania. So it's a fallacy that rattling is effective only in the brush country of the desert Southwest. On the contrary, rattling will work anywhere!

## FIGHTING BEHAVIOR OF BUCKS

To understand the phenomenal success many hunters are enjoying in rattling-in bucks, it first

Peter Fiduccia, host of TV's "Woods 'n Waters" show, with proof positive that the effectiveness of antler rattling is not restricted to Texas where the technique originated. These splendid bucks were taken in New York.

is necessary to clarify certain aspects of the social lives of male deer.

When bucks fight, it is a spectacle to behold, but genuine brawls between whitetail bucks are actually quite rare. An all-out donnybrook usually only takes place when a dominant buck, for one reason or another, leaves his own breeding territory, where his hierarchal ranking is well established, and ventures into an adjacent area inhabited by another buck that is likewise of clearly superior ranking in his own social group.

When this happens, both animals become enraged at the other's presence. They engage in quick charges and violent antler clashing. As their rage intensifies, their neck muscles bulge, and they grind their antlers together and gyrate their shoulders, each trying to push the other back upon his haunches. Ultimately, one of the gladiators accepts defeat and timidly slinks away or is chased from the vicinity by the victor.

There is no mistaking the arena where a genuine whitetail buck fight has just taken place. Often as much as twenty-five square yards of sod and forest duff are torn up, and the air is usually filled with the pungent aroma of tarsal scent. And because their fever-pitched fighting

**Episodes of violent fighting among bucks are rare and usually occur only when a dominant buck leaves his breeding area and enters that of another dominant male. These two rivals did not survive the encounter.**

episodes normally reach abnormally high metabolic levels, causing the animals to void themselves, the ground is also likely to be urine-dampened and littered with feces.

I know several photographers and cinematographers who earn full-time livelihoods filming animal behavior, and all of them claim that in their entire professional careers they've observed legitimate buck fights on only a handful of occasions. What most hunters actually witness when they report having seen two bucks fighting is not really fighting at all, but the far more commonplace occurrence known as sparring.

Sparring among bucks is an attempt to sort out who's who in the social order, and such episodes don't even begin to take on the characteristics of a vicious encounter. Rather, sparring mostly consists of posturing, bluffing and other mild-mannered attempts at intimidation. To be sure, there's likely to be some antler meshing between the two animals, but it is invariably very toned-down in terms of aggressive intent; the bucks merely bring their heads together, engage their racks, push until a bit of resistance is met, twist their necks several times and then quickly separate. As often as not,

When hunters claim to have seen deer fighting, what they've most likely seen was brief, mild-mannered sparring among males attempting to establish their places in the social hierarchy.

they may then return to feeding within scant yards of each other.

This shadowboxing prelude continues until such time as the seasonal flow of testosterone begins to heighten in mature animals, causing them to assume their designated positions in the local hierarchy and take encounters with other males far more seriously. But by that time, most mature bucks have long since staked out their own individual breeding grounds, where they simply do not have many opportunities for interactions with each other; hence, the infrequent occurrence of genuine fighting activities.

The significance of all of this explains why many hunters are enjoying tremendous success rattling-in bucks while other hunters are having so little success that many of them even claim rattling isn't very effective.

In my opinion, these latter hunters are making the mistake of rattling in the wrong location and at the wrong time of year. In addition—

and most importantly—they rattle too loudly, too intensely, and for too long, thus simulating genuine buck fights, which I've already noted are relatively rare. As a result, most of the bucks that hear their rattling are undoubtedly spooked and slip away unseen.

Keep in mind that when a buck hears the clash of antlers in the distance, he's already well aware of his own ranking in the local pecking order. And since our deer herds are cropped so heavily each year, and there just aren't great numbers of mature trophies in any given region, the buck likely has a subordinate place on the totem pole.

The hypothetical buck we're describing may indeed be a semi-mature 2½-year-old deer sporting a decent eight-point rack. But he's certainly not going to respond to the apparent sound of a couple of five-year-old males bent upon killing each other! After all, why should he risk humiliation and defeat, and perhaps

The cardinal sin committed by most hunters who take up antler rattling
is rattling too loudly and too long. This buck, scared away by loud rattling, was probably afraid of encountering more dominant animals.

even a serious goring, by stepping into the ring where two obviously superior animals are engaged in heated battle?

## RATTLING TECHNIQUES

The best antlers for rattling should be fresh (less than ten years old). They should be stored indoors when not in use. Picked-up sheds that have become weathered and bleached have lost most of their tonal qualities. I don't like antlers that are overly large and heavy as they're a burden to carry. Incidentally, you don't even have to use whitetail antlers! Modest-size antlers from mule deer or blacktails work equally well, as do the new synthetic antlers now on the market.

It's wise to perform a bit of surgery on antlers before attempting to use them. First, file or grind down the many little bumps and protrusions at the bases of the beams, and even remove the brow tines if they are situated in such a way that holding the antlers is uncomfortable. Doing these two things will help prevent your hands from getting sore while rattling. Then drill a hole through the base of each antler so you can connect them with a length of cord and sling them over your shoulder in the field.

The easiest way to describe the rattling sounds you want to make to duplicate the sounds of bucks sparring is to imagine a flamenco dancer clicking his/her castanets in slow motion. Try to recreate that sound with the

**Noel Feather of Sterling, Illinois, the only hunter to have successfully rattled-in and taken three Boone & Crockett whitetails: "Use fresh antlers for rattling, not bleached sheds you've found while scouting. They don't have to be overly large but should comfortably fit your hands."**

The most effective rattling technique, especially when you first arrive on stand, is meshing the antlers and then gently shaking your hands to produce a clicking sound like that of a flamenco dancer's castanets. This is precisely the sound of sparring bucks.

antlers. Do not loudly and repeatedly clash the antlers together, at least not at first, or you'll spook away bucks in the vicinity. Simply mesh the antlers together and then gently shake your hands as though they were wet and you were shaking off excess water before reaching for a towel. And now and then barely tick the tips of the tines together.

Timing is indeed important to give any buck in the region ample opportunity to hear the rattling and then respond to it by traveling in your direction. I suggest rattling for several minutes, waiting fifteen minutes, then rattling again and waiting another fifteen minutes before moving to a new location.

I emphasize this because the great shortcoming of many hunters is enacting an acceptable rattling routine but then abandoning their posts if a buck doesn't immediately show up. Sometimes a buck will indeed charge to your location in a matter of mere seconds, but usually it takes at least fifteen minutes for him to appear, and just as frequently it's not until after you've finished your second sequence that he shows any interest.

## Best Rattling Times

Hunters enjoy the greatest rattling success three or four weeks prior to the peak of the rut, when bucks are sexually frustrated. They've long since been eager to breed, but does are not yet fully receptive. Therefore, when a buck hears what he interprets to be two other male deer sparring, he'll rush to the scene to make his own dominant ranking known. By doing this, when the first of the does in the region do begin coming into heat, that buck will have long since asserted his right to be the one to do the breeding.

North of the Mason-Dixon line, the pre-rut period is generally the last two weeks of October and the first week in November; in the Deep South, rattling may be effective from early December through January.

## Setting up for Action

Murry Burnham, who manufactures wildlife calls in Marble Falls, Texas, is a seasoned pro when it comes to rattling. And one thing he considers far more important than the actual cadence or rhythm involved in rattling is how and where a hunter sets up to perform his theatrics.

"Be sure to select a vantage point on high ground," Murry advises, "because an unexplainable quirk of nature is that most animal species that respond to various types of calls are extremely difficult to entice downhill. Deer, especially, are far more inclined to respond if they are able to travel uphill or at least remain on the same level of elevation."

Antler rattling can be done from a tree stand, or on the ground, and each approach has its own inherent advantages and disadvantages.

Remember that when a buck responds to rattling, you become the hunted! The buck will be making a diligent attempt to pinpoint the source of the rattling noise and to make visual contact with what he perceives are other bucks encroaching upon his breeding territory. Moreover, since deer don't live in trees, a responding buck will be focusing his attention upon the ground-level terrain ahead of him.

Consequently, a hunter who is perched in a tree stand has a much better chance of going undetected than a hunter who is rattling from the ground. Also, from an elevated position, it's much easier to look down and through cover to survey your surroundings. This can be critical because when a buck is responding, you'll want to see him early enough—when he's still in the distance—to have sufficient time to stop rattling, set down the antlers and reach for your bow or gun.

I've had several experiences rattling from ground level where surrounding brush blocked my view, only to see a buck that had sneaked in unannounced and was standing only yards away staring at me. In such situations, there's simply no time to plan for a shot because even a blink on your part will spook the deer.

A distinct disadvantage of rattling from a tree stand is that, unless you've prepared in advance and hung portable stands in numerous places, you are locked into one specific location. Conversely, when rattling from ground level, you can move around freely throughout the day.

## Fine-tuning Your Technique

If you plan to rattle from a tree stand during the early-morning hours and then again at dusk, there is no better location than in the vicinity of scrapes. During the pre-rut period, when bucks are anxiously waiting for the first does to come into estrus, they will not tolerate other bucks near their scrapes. Since a scrape can be considered a type of "bait" that a buck has set out to attract a doe, he doesn't want to risk the possibility of another buck breeding that doe.

However, if a hunter plans to rattle during the midday hours, which can be equally exciting, the best location to set up is not around scrapes but in the vicinity of a buck bedding area. Just be sure to set up downwind of the bedding area so that your scent is not permitted to drift into the very path from which you expect a buck to approach.

Generally, I prefer my antler rattling performance to be a solo endeavor during an early-morning vigil in a tree stand, and crisp, cold mornings seem to be the most conducive to

During the early morning and late afternoon hours, rattle in the vicinity of scrapes. But during mid-day, set up downwind of a buck's bedding area.

Teaming up with a partner is the most enjoyable and exciting way to rattle-in deer. Always have the shooter up front and the rattler behind. When a deer approaches the rattling, he should walk past the lead hunter and provide an easy broadside shot.

buck activity during the pre-rut period.

In fact, when a hunter first climbs into a stand in pre-dawn darkness, there's no telling how close a buck may be, and if there is a buck close by, the sudden loud clash of antlers being rattled is almost certain to alarm him. So, as mentioned earlier, always begin rattling softly. Just barely tickle the antlers, wait fifteen minutes, and then gradually increase the volume so the simulated sparring sound will travel farther.

Teaming up with a partner also is effective and enables two hunters to move around and cover many square miles of terrain during the day. In using a teamwork approach, the hunter doing the rattling should position himself forty to fifty yards behind his partner. This way, when a responding buck rivets his attention upon the exact location where the rattling sound is coming from, and then begins closing the distance, he is likely to walk past the hunter waiting up front. Often the lead hunter has an easy close-range broadside shot at a slowly sneaking animal that is completely unaware of his presence.

# 12

## How Experts Call Deer

Calling animals such as deer is not really new at all. Two centuries ago hunters were already using rudimentary types of mouth calls to lure antlered game into shooting range. But it wasn't until the late 1970s that biologists began intensively studying the vocalizations whitetails use in their social interactions.

Among the most notable of the scientific investigations were those conducted by Dr. Thomas Atkeson and Dr. Larry Marchington at the University of Georgia. They made tape recordings of penned deer which were associated with specific types of behavior. Since then, numerous manufacturers have applied this knowledge to making a wide array of calls that are far more sophisticated than our ancestors could have ever dreamed of using.

### GRUNT CALLS

Grunt calls are far and away the most popular, but the great shortcoming among novice hunters is blowing into them too loudly and too forcefully. It's much better to sound like a wimp.

Take what happened last year in Kentucky's

**Whitetails are very vocal animals. They bleat, blat, grunt, whistle, snort, mew and make numerous other sounds to communicate with other deer.**

**Biologists have used special audio equipment to record the vocalizations of deer and predict their behavior.**

Land-Between-the-Lakes region when I attempted to grunt a respectable eight-pointer into shooting range. At first, the deer registered a mild interest by jerking his head upright and cupping his ears in my direction. This stand-off, in which the animal remained about eighty yards away, lasted about five minutes, and when it became clear the deer wasn't going to come any closer, I tried to coax him with a series of bolder, louder challenges. At that, the deer protruded his tongue laterally out of the side of his mouth, lowered his head and slinked away. Right then, when the buck exhibited this typical fear response, I knew I had blown it.

"You'll attract more flies with just a little sugar than with a lot of vinegar," my partner Harold Knight later explained.

"One of the biggest mistakes made by deer hunters is being too loud and aggressive with a grunt call," David Hale added. "That only serves to intimidate most bucks and scare them away."

Later, back at Harold and David's factory in Cadiz, Kentucky, where they manufacture some of the highest-quality animal calls on the market, I was shown their latest video on calling deer and was amazed to see what really goes on in the vocal lives of whitetails.

"When attempting to call a wary whitetail buck, you have to create an aura that makes him feel comfortable," Harold Knight emphasizes. "Remember, whitetails are gregarious, social animals; they adhere to rigid pecking orders and mutually respect each other's rank. But most important of all, keep in mind that in any deer population, the vast majority of the bucks are subordinates. Only a few—the very largest and oldest—achieve dominant status. Therefore, if you grunt too often, too loudly, and too forcefully, the only thing you'll accomplish is scaring most of the male deer."

What Harold Knight says makes good sense. After all, who wants to intentionally risk a fight with a bully, suffer a bruised ego and maybe even receive battle scars? Yet that is exactly the type of intimidation a buck may feel he's in for if he responds to a call supposedly being made by a superior animal.

"On the other hand," David Hale explains, "imagine the weakling on the beach who, by his very presence, invites trouble. That's the kind of illusion you want to create in the deer woods. You want to be a wimp deer that is very low on the hierarchal totem pole so that virtually any other buck in the vicinity will feel confident he can give you a whipping."

While a grunt call may draw the interest of a buck almost anytime during the fall and winter, there is a specific period of time just before does begin coming into estrus when bucks are the most vocal. This is the pre-rut when bucks and does play a cat and mouse game in preparation for breeding, during which a buck's desire to mate reaches feverish heights.

The scenario unfolds with the buck charging after the doe in a stiff-legged gait with his nose tight to the ground. All the while he grunts, trying to persuade the doe to stop and stand. There is a unique tonal quality to the buck's grunting, produced by staccato exhaling and inhaling. Liken it to the sound of a person trying to jog and talk at the same time. It's this breathless excitation in the buck's grunting that attracts other bucks within earshot and causes them to rush to the scene in an attempt to horn in on the action.

Harold Knight and David Hale, when video taping and audio taping deer, discovered that this unique grunting sound cannot be reproduced by simply blowing (exhaling) into a conventional grunt tube. So they reinvented the grunt call. Their advanced model, which is appropriately called The Hyper-Ventilator, is the only call on the market that allows a hunter to inhale and exhale through the same end of the tube and produce the breathless sound of a buck just moments before he breeds with a doe.

When using a grunt call, more is not always better. Whenever you're calling, you are broadcasting your location. The more you call, the greater the chance a deer will become aware of your presence, and when that happens it's all over.

"One of the most critical aspects of using a grunt call is knowing when to stop," David Hale points out. "If you can see a buck in the distance, perhaps seventy-five yards away, and he's obviously responding to your call by slowly moving in your direction, put the danged call down! It has performed its function and now you should let him come the rest of the way in of his own accord. Make him hunt you! Only if the deer turns and begins moving in the opposite direction should you attempt to coax him back."

It's also worth noting that the volume of the calling effort should always be considerably toned down as the deer approaches closer and closer. Not only will grunting too loudly make it easier for a buck to peg your location but, as I mentioned before, it is likely to spook him.

## BLEAT CALLS

Every serious hunter should always have several calls in his possession. His mainstay will undoubtedly be a Hyper-Ventilator grunt tube, yet there are many times when a bleat call, which simulates a young deer in distress, will

The newest and most advanced version of the grunt call allows you to inhale and exhale through the same end of the tube to produce the breathless excitation of a buck tending a near-estrous doe.

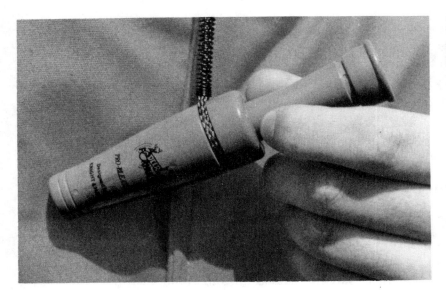

**Every hunter needs a bleat call that simulates a young deer in distress.**

bring in the biggest buck of all. If that sounds like an unlikely situation, consider how this particular vocalization influences whitetails.

In the animal kingdom, which includes domesticated animals as well as wildlife, females which have previously given birth at least once feel an instinctive need to protect the young of their species, even if a given individual is not their own offspring.

"One time I was sitting in a tree stand and from about 250 yards away watching a doe with two yearlings by her side which I am sure were hers," relates Will Primos of Primos Wild Game Calls (P.O. Box 12785, Jackson, MS 39236). "When I bleated with my call, she immediately threw her head up high and became instantly alert as she looked straight in my direction. When I bleated a second time, she left her two offspring and charged straight toward me on a dead run, even though the distress call I was simulating couldn't have been from one of her own young."

Although a bleat call brings in more does than anything else, bucks quite often respond as well. When a mature, dominant buck is taken through the assistance of a bleat call, however, it is not the call that proves to be his undoing but rather his libido. That's because once a doe

begins climbing to the zenith of her estrous cycle, there is nothing a hunter can do to coax a tending buck away from her side.

Faced with this frustrating situation, most hunters either throw up their hands in despair or continue to grind away with their antlers and blow on their grunt call. Yet there's an easy solution at hand.

Simply put, *if you cannot call in a rut-crazed buck, call the doe instead and you can be sure the buck will follow.*

Many hunters restrict their antler rattling and grunting to the pre-rut preparation period, and as the peak of the rut nears use only their bleat calls. Even though a doe might be right in the middle of her estrous cycle and is repeatedly being serviced by an amorous buck, she still feels the maternal instinct to come to the assistance of a fawn or yearling which she perceives to be injured or suffering from some other distress.

Incidentally, Harold Knight and David Hale designed their bleat call only after they came upon a young deer caught in a fence and audio-taped its frantic vocalizations; that tape is available in cassette form (Knight & Hale Game Calls, Box 468, Cadiz, KY 42211) so a hunter can listen to it and master the use of his bleat call.

If you are sitting in a tree stand or ground

Whenever you buy any type of deer call, find out if the manufacturer offers an instructional audio tape. When you can hear experts mimicking deer sounds, it's easier to learn how to use a call.

blind and there are no deer anywhere in sight, blow on the call about once every twenty minutes. Don't blow any more frequently than this because on a calm day deer can hear this call up to a half mile away, and even if they respond immediately it will take them a bit of time to travel the distance.

Harold Knight advises: "If no deer are in sight, blow your bleat call as loud as possible. Don't be afraid to put on some theatrics with a lot of intense wailing and feeling. If you've ever heard a live fawn tangled in a fence or being pulled down by a coyote, it screams its lungs out and almost makes your hair stand on end. That's the very type of intensity and volume you want to project with your call."

"On the other hand," Will Primos adds, "if you have a deer in sight in the distance, use a slightly reduced volume by cupping your palm over the end of the call and blowing less forcefully, yet do continue to embellish your calling

with plenty of soft cries of distress."

Incidentally, one of Will Primos' latest innovations on behalf of bowhunters is grunt calls and bleat calls that can be held securely in the side of the mouth while simultaneously drawing a bowstring and releasing an arrow; this idea eliminates the hand movements associated with raising and lowering a call to the mouth and thus possibly alerting a deer that is very close to one's stand.

## FINE-TUNING YOUR CALLING

From my experience, using a grunt call or bleat call is best accomplished in mildly windy weather. True, your call won't carry as far as on a dead calm day, but there are other advantages that fall in your favor.

The noise of the wind itself, and the associated sounds of rustling leaves and clacking tree branches, interfere with a deer's effective use of

One of the newest innovations is a call a bowhunter can hold in his mouth while coming to full draw. This eliminates hand-to-mouth movements that might spook a deer.

its sense of hearing. Consequently, an approaching deer quite often becomes confused over where the call originated. If it's a buck, it expects to encounter a rival buck doing the grunting, and if it's a doe it expects to find a young deer in distress. When the deer fails to find the source of the call, it begins to wander erratically, apparently presuming the deer it heard is still farther ahead, or off to one side or the other. In any event, when a responding deer becomes momentarily disoriented, it becomes careless and makes mistakes. This gives you a

slight edge that may translate into a clear shot at a totally unsuspecting animal.

It's also a sly ruse to team up with a partner to do your calling. Many hunters already take this approach when rattling antlers, but few ever think to employ a team effort when using mouth calls.

The setup is simple. Just have the shooter positioned about fifty yards ahead of the caller. A deer attempting to find the source of the call is likely to walk right past the forward hunter and provide a point-blank shot. After a half-

A mouse-squeaker call is effective when a deer is feeding in waist-high grass and all you can see is the ridge of his back. Just one squeak and he'll crane his head for a look-see, providing a clear neck shot.

Any time you glimpse a deer up ahead just stepping into cover, try a predator call. Chances are he'll turn and come back to investigate.

hour of unsuccessful calling, move several hundred yards and try again, and then still again, throughout the entire day. During the brief pre-rut period, you can even combine rattling *and* grunting to bring in bucks.

## WHISTLING FOR DEER

"When a running deer hears a shrill whistle, its first inclination is to slam to a halt until such time as it is able to use its ears, eyes or nose to identify the source of the sound before taking further evasive action. To continue moving, without making this identification, would incur the risk of running right into the lap of danger," explains Brad Harris of Lohman Game Calls (P.O. Box 220, Neosho, MO 64850).

That's why Lohman developed a new concept in calls with their Whistlin' Deer Stopper, which is specifically intended for use when a hunter inadvertently spooks a deer out of cover and it begins bounding away, or when a hunter playing the role of stander during the course of a deer drive sees a buck running pell-mell through his area.

"The logic behind this call is easy to understand," Harris says. "Conventional whistling with the lips pursed together is an age-old, proven method for stopping moving deer in their tracks. The pitch is so much higher and uncharacteristic of anything deer customarily hear in the woodlands that it confuses them and brings them to a stop to see what's going on. My problem, which is shared by countless other hunters, is that I cannot produce a high-pitched whistle that's loud enough."

Yet that is exactly what's needed if the wind is blowing, or the deer is far away, or the animal itself is making plenty of noise crashing away through dry cover. Lohman's Whistlin' Deer Stopper is perfect for any of these situations because both its volume and pitch carry well beyond 100 yards, even under the most adverse conditions.

## THE PREDATOR-CALL GAMBIT

Like antler rattling, using mouth-blown calls originated in the brush country of south Texas. Yet, strangely, deer were *not* the intended target species but rather an unexpected surprise that began arriving on the scene when varmint hunters were using predator calls for species such as coyotes, foxes and bobcats.

Why a whitetail would eagerly respond to a call that sounds like a small mammal in distress, such as an injured rabbit, is conjecture and something only the deer themselves could explain. But the fact that they do engage in such bizarre behavior is precisely why many hunters around the country now integrate a wide variety of predator calls into their various advanced deer hunting strategies.

Murry Burnham of Burnham Game Calls (Marble Falls, TX 78654) is a classic example, for he never goes deer hunting without his screaming rabbit call in his pocket.

"At first," Murry explained, "I just used the rabbit call only toward the end of each vigil on stand, right before I was ready to give up for the day and go home, as sort of a last-ditch measure. But after several years of noticing how it aroused the curiosity of deer, many of which I took during those final moments of waiting on stand, I began using it more frequently. In fact, our company now even sells predator calls on cassette tapes which can be played in portable, battery-operated recorders in the field for the utmost in realism.

"The exciting thing is you never know what's going to show up. And I guarantee it will raise bristles on the back of your neck to suddenly see a bobcat stalking you, for then it's patently clear *you* are the one being hunted!" Burnham said. "Yet other times it's a coyote that comes in, or a doe or small buck. In fact, it seems as if young bucks are the most likely to show an interest in a predator call."

I have used a mouse-squeaker call with success on big bucks in several different states. When a buck is slowly feeding along in waist-high brush or vegetation and you can see only the ridge of his back, the squeaking noise will make him raise his head every time, to provide an easy neck shot.

And one time I was stillhunting on a logging trail through a climax forest when up ahead I glimpsed the rump of a deer just as it was step-ping off the trail into the timber. I couldn't tell whether it was a buck or doe, so I stopped immediately, raised my rifle to my shoulder, squeaked two or three times, and the deer came right back into the open to investigate. I credit that eight-pointer to my call because otherwise he would have been long gone.

# 13

# Decoy Your Deer

Any hunter who has pursued deer for more than two decades accumulates a storehouse of exciting memories, and I am certainly no different. In fact, one experience stands out among all others, and nothing will probably ever top it even if I'm granted another twenty years in my favorite whitetail woods.

I had placed a buck decoy on a slightly elevated knoll along the leading edge of a forest. Not long after, from a tree stand, I began a combination rattling/grunting routine and almost immediately heard a crashing of brush and popping of brittle branches as an eight-point buck bolted from the woods.

When the buck reached the open edge he didn't even pause to check things out. He just kept going, full-steam ahead, with his rack held low and his dagger-like bay tines aimed straight forward. The deer crossed the opening in a flash and with a vicious lunge rammed right into my McKenzie buck decoy and knocked it over. Only then did the animal finally discover he'd been the victim of a hoax and vanished, leaving me soaking wet with sweat and short of breath.

It's my guess that deer decoys were born in 1985. This was when the Ohio Division of Wildlife began making a concerted effort to crack down on road hunters and other opportunists who keep loaded guns in their vehicles in the hope they'll see a deer along the berm or in an open field.

"We had a full-body mount made of an eight-point whitetail buck," wildlife official Larry Harmon explained, "and then we placed it in strategic locations visible from highways. Conservation officers on stakeouts then began nabbing violators who shot at the deer from their vehicles. Wide media exposure was given the arrests so that they would serve as a deterrent to others who might be tempted to engage in such illegal hunting practices."

Paradoxically enough, the mounted buck was named "Memorex," after the television commercial promoting the audio recording tape which supposedly produces the most realistic copy. Wildlife officer Chip Gross told me, "We want would-be game law violators who see a deer near any road in the state to wonder if it's real or a Memorex?"

Later that same year, while sitting in a tree

After hearing antler rattling and grunting, this buck bolted from the woods into an open field and, seeing a McKenzie decoy, mistook it for a rival buck. The buck charged the decoy and gored it repeatedly before realizing he'd been duped.

**Is it a real, live deer or is it Memorex?**

stand in Ohio, I began softly chuckling as I thought about the novel approach of using a counterfeit deer in the enforcement of wildlife regulations. But what especially amused me was that I was now using the very same technique in reverse. I had situated a deer decoy in an open meadow before me, but instead of attempting to catch a poacher or road hunter I was hoping it would lure a nice buck into range.

Of course, duck and goose hunters have used representative decoys for generations, as have a smattering of other sportsmen after doves, crows, and of late even turkeys. More recently, the most revolutionary use of decoys—an advanced strategy of the highest order—is for whitetail deer, but you don't need a large number as in the pursuit of certain other game species; just one is enough.

## WHY DECOYS WORK

Like wildfowl, whitetails are gregarious animals. In fact, they are so socially oriented that they establish a well-defined pecking order within

their ranks. Yet whitetails also are shy, furtive creatures that like to cling to the safety of dark shadows and dense cover. But when they see one or more other deer standing in an open place, they often join them. It was this habit I was counting on as I maintained my vigil in a tree stand.

I had previously pegged the routines of several deer. In late afternoon they usually left their beds in a distant canebrake and slipped through a crabapple thicket almost to the edge of a red clover meadow where they'd eventually begin filling their paunches. I was growing exasperated because the deer always hung back within the leading edge of the cover until late evening dusk had settled in and shooting light was almost gone. Moreover, there was an eight-point buck in the band, and he always was the very last to leave his security cover and begin feeding. So, on a whim, I had decided to experiment by placing my 3-D bowhunting target in the open field. This particular target was made by Delta Industries (117 E. Kenwood, Reinbeck, IA 50669; price, around $115).

When the sun settled on the horizon—but with ample shooting light still remaining—I was amazed how much the backlighted 3-D target looked like a real deer. But it was when three does entered the meadow, heading directly toward the decoy, that my heart really began hammering. They were not just casually walking but actually bouncing along in a loping gait with no apparent shyness whatsoever. Moments later, the eight-pointer followed quickly behind!

I would like to claim that the reason my arrow flew harmlessly over the deer's back was due to a variety of technical reasons beyond my control. But if the truth be known, the scenario of rapidly unfolding and completely unexpected events took me entirely by surprise and I simply muffed the shot.

In any event, if not venison and hefty antlers, at least I took home a bit of valuable knowledge; namely, whitetail deer can indeed be successfully decoyed. Since then, I've also learned that the number of ways they can be duped in this manner is limited only by one's understanding of whitetail behavior.

These techniques are so effective, however, that in those regions where the firearm season is brief and the woodlands are crowded, the use of a decoy could pose a distinct safety problem. Therefore, I strongly recommend their use only by bowhunters or gun hunters in sparsely populated areas or on large tracts of private land. And even then, for safety reasons, tie an inexpensive orange vest around the midsection of the decoy while carrying it to your stand location. Once there, remove the carrying strap and orange vest and hide them in nearby cover.

## TYPES OF DECOYS

Now, let's consider the actual decoys themselves. The most realistic kind is made by a taxidermist. The primary obstacle is the cost—about $700. Perhaps two or three regular hunting partners could split the cost.

Decoys are effective because deer are gregarious animals.

Some decoys have real antlers, glass taxidermy eyes and even a tanned deer's tail.

The taxidermist should be instructed to affix the antlers so they can be easily removed. One method is to drive a single screw through each antler burr into the skullplate or mannequin block. The reason for this is that, under certain circumstances to be discussed later, you'll want to use a buck decoy, yet other times you'll want to remove the antlers in order to use a doe decoy.

A more viable alternative is the Deer-Coy made by Harry Brunett's Montana Critter Company (4405 Buttercup Lane, Missoula, MT 59802). Although this decoy is made of polyurethane foam, it is extremely lifelike due to its glass eyes, real detachable antlers and an authentic, tanned whitetail tail. The Deer-Coy is currently priced at about $600.

Then there is the Duffel Decoy, an inexpensive model that is collapsible. The Duffel Decoy is made of a leatherlike material that can be rolled up to about the size of a small sleeping bag. It weighs about one pound, has removable foam antlers, costs about $85, and is available through Delta Industries (address given earlier). To use, just unroll and pop into shape, then stand it up on two short support stakes pressed into the ground.

It's important to note that with deer decoys, like most other things in life, you pretty much get what you pay for. A full-body mount of a previously live deer may succeed in luring whitetails to within scant yards to investigate. Conversely, when using a commercially manufactured decoy, the closer the deer approaches the more likely it will eventually realize it has been duped by a counterfeit.

Therefore, by way of illustration, a full-body mount of a doe placed near a scrape may allow a hunter in a nearby tree stand to eventually be rewarded with a mere five-yard shot at a responding buck. On the other hand, a factory-made decoy works best when trying to catch the eye of a deer from a distance.

## DECOYS AFIELD

Two decoys I'm presently using are 3-D foam archery targets which can be quickly disassembled for easy transportation in a vehicle. Both have removable antlers.

One is made by McKenzie Supply Company (P.O. Box 480, Granite Quarry, NC 28072). Support rods emanating from the legs, which are easily pressed into the earth, allow the decoy to be placed virtually anywhere on short notice, or the rods can attach to a base stand. This is a relatively small decoy with a small six-point rack; the price is around $90. I have installed two eyebolts along the length of the back to attach a shoulder strap that allows me to carry the decoy afield. This is the decoy I use mostly for bowhunting when I want a buck to come close without feeling intimidated by a larger deer.

My other favorite archery target used as a decoy is made by Timberline (P.O. Box 667,

Williston, ND 58801). This decoy is much larger, has a ten-point rack and comes with its own self-supporting plywood base, yet the entire affair is light enough to carry short distances afield. I use this decoy for rifle hunting, particularly in open country where it can be identified at long range.

## RATTLING UP A BUCK

There are many ways buck and doe decoys can be used, but they are unquestionably the most effective when rattling antlers during the rutting season.

When a buck responds to the sound of antlers meshing in the distance, the animal invariably expects to find one of two things. If

The McKenzie decoy is lightweight and very portable. Note carrying strap attached to eyebolts on the front shoulder and rump.

The magnum size of the Timberline decoy makes it ideal for use in very large meadows where there is long-range visibility.

The Doe-Coy attaches to a tree trunk and provides a visual stimulus designed to lure a buck out of distant cover.

**Decoys work best in conjunction with antler rattling. This is the Delta 3-D archery target the author often uses as a decoy.**

he is the dominant buck in that neck of the woods, he expects to find two subordinate males jousting with each other and a nearby estrous doe in waiting. In this case, he'll come in fast, making his hierarchal ranking known, drive the younger deer away, and then attempt to get cozy with the female.

Yet if the responding buck is a subordinate animal, he doesn't know quite what to expect at the scene of the antler rattling. He may very well come upon two males that are even lower than he on the totem pole, or he may find two superior animals attempting to sort out their differences; consequently, he'll come in slowly and suspiciously, hanging back a safe distance until he has fully appraised the situation.

This is why hunters who rattle antlers report oftentimes entirely different responses from approaching bucks.

Moreover, whitetails are extremely adept at pinpointing the exact location of antler rattling sounds and if, upon their arrival, they see no other deer at the scene they immediately become very suspicious and either remain at a cautious distance or altogether evaporate. Therefore, a decoy of either a buck or doe provides the responding buck with the visual confirmation so vitally necessary to lure him in to bow or rifle range.

## BUCK OR DOE DECOY?

To decide whether to use a buck decoy, or with antlers removed, a doe decoy, let the season and type of hunting dictate your choice.

For example, if my stand or blind is situated along the edge of an alfalfa meadow, and the rut is not in progress, I'm undoubtedly waiting for deer to come to a favorite food source. And, knowing in advance they might wait until it is almost dark before stepping out into the open, I'll station a *doe* decoy in the meadow. Throughout the year whitetails live in a matriarchal society, and it is therefore always the adult does, not the younger deer or bucks of any ages, which are the decision-makers. In a band of deer, it is typically a mature doe that enters an open feeding area first and by her presence or through her lead tells others still hanging back in their security cover that it's safe to venture forth. Of course, this is not a rigid rule, but it occurs often enough to warrant using a doe decoy.

The doe decoy I use most often for this kind of work is the Redi-Doe (Flambeau Products, P.O. Box 97, Middlefield, OH 44062). This durable plastic decoy is extremely lifelike and allows the hunter to adjust the position of the ears and head. Also, all body parts can be disassembled and stowed inside the body trunk for easy portability.

Doe decoys also are recommended during the peak of the rut when amorous bucks are tirelessly checking their scrapes. Now is when a bedded doe decoy situated in an open clearing

These Redi-Does, by Flambeau Products, are ideal for use in food plots where their presence may give a shy buck the confidence to venture into the open.

These are bedded doe decoys by Feather-Flex. Does frequently lie down during the breeding season to facilitate conception, and this pose tells nearby bucks they are in heat.

can be a dynamite technique, for two important reasons. First, a bedded doe is a relaxed deer, and this instills confidence and reassurance in a buck that sees the decoy. But also, does which have just recently been bred commonly lay down in open areas because the bedding posture, with body-weight pressure exerted upon the lower abdomen, helps to facilitate conception. This posture draws the interest of bucks which may be curious if the doe will allow subsequent breeding.

An excellent bedded doe decoy is the Feather-Flex (1655 Swan Lake Rd, Bossier City, LA 71111). This is a soft, extruded shell decoy made of polyethylene foam that is very realistic. It also is extremely lightweight, weighing only 12 ounces, and can be rolled up and stowed in a small duffle bag.

The prime time to use a buck decoy is very early in the season; in the North this means the months of September and October, and in the South it means November and December. This is well before does customarily begin coming into heat and so, for the time being, the bucks inhabiting the same general region engage in sparring with each other in order to determine their place in the breeding establishment. Very few scrapes are yet in evidence at this time, but in scouting the terrain you're certain to discover numerous antler rubs on saplings as these tie in directly with the animals' rapidly developing pecking order.

The best place to station a buck decoy is in an open field or small clearing bordering a deeply forested region, or along a well-established rub line, but in any case in the vicinity of the first-appearing and largest rubs of the season, as these are the work of the largest and most mature males in the area. Then either rattle antlers or just patiently wait for the return of the resident buck which made the rubs. You might even want to use your grunt call at this time.

I have a sly trick I use with either buck or doe decoys. I stow a few feet of white toilet paper and some tape in my pocket and then, on location, attach a one-foot section of the paper onto the deer's rump so that it occasionally flutters in the wind to simulate a real deer flicking its tail.

In addition to decoys serving the purpose of bringing bucks into shooting range, either by giving them a false sense of security so they'll step into open places, or by sexually arousing them to the presence of a ready doe, or by challenging their hierarchal ranking, they have another equally important function.

A decoy occupies an approaching deer's attention and diverts it from the hunter. Although this is an especially critical concern of bowhunters, most gun hunters are detected by a deer before they are able to get off a telling shot. But all of this bears a note of qualification.

Never place a decoy facing your tree stand or ground blind because a deer might look at what the decoy is looking at. Also, when bowhunting, always place your decoy in relation to your stand so that a buck must walk past you to approach the decoy.

In all likelihood there are a number of other situations in which an enterprising hunter might find a deer decoy effective. But using decoys is so new that hunters are still trying to learn what works and what doesn't.

Nevertheless, one thing is certain. By understanding weather conditions, wind and thermals, we've found ways to reduce a deer's ability to use its keen sense of smell in detecting our presence. And through the use of rattling antlers and various types of calls, we're now able to deceive their acute hearing abilities. And as additional uses for decoys begin to evolve, in order to play tricks on the eyes of deer, we'll have effectively countered the three senses they use to elude legions of hunters every year. None of this will make deer hunting easy, by any stretch of the imagination, but I like to think that maybe it will even up the odds a bit.

# 14

# Weather and Whitetails

When Larry Miller walked through the cabin door, he looked like a bedraggled, half-drowned cat someone had just rescued from a deep well.

For the better part of the week we had been sharing a rustic cabin on his brother's farm in northern Michigan, and after four consecutive days of unrelenting rain we were both ready to throw in the towel, but only if we could find a dry one.

"This hunt is proving to be one of the biggest challenges I've ever undertaken," Larry remarked while standing in a growing puddle of his own drippings. "But the deer hunting isn't the challenging part. It's the need to return to the cabin repeatedly for an hour to hang sopping-wet gear before the fireplace."

Then Miller began shucking clothes, one layer at a time, in search of something still dry underneath. He never found it. Nevertheless, by week's end he had taken an eight-pointer while I had meanwhile collected a sleek forkhorn, both by stillhunting in a manner I'll describe later.

## WHAT CONTROLS DEER ACTIVITY?

There is no question that hunting pressure influences deer behavior. The type of food available, and its location, also influences their activity. And the rutting period certainly affects their movements. Yet on a day to day basis, weather is a far greater factor in governing deer behavior. This gives a serious hunter a certain advantage, for he can analyze weather conditions and determine what deer are likely to do before the deer themselves even think about doing it.

One way of accomplishing this is with a small weather radio. Some very good ones are no larger than a coffee mug and cost less than $20, and since they are battery operated you can take them to deer camp. These radios are tuned to only one channel, that of the National Weather Service, and forecasts for your specific region, no matter where you happen to be at the time, are updated every five minutes.

While unsettled weather sharply curtails deer activity, the first sign of clearing, calm weather puts all deer on their feet and, usually, headed for the nearest food source.

How does one interpret such forecasts? Well, basically, since whitetails are skittish, tense, extremely wary creatures, it stands to reason that unstable weather, which prevents them from using their senses effectively, tells them the most prudent decision is to dive into cover and not even blink. Conversely, it is calm, stable weather, which permits them to use their senses efficiently, as well as pacifying them and encouraging them to engage in a myriad of activities.

Regular partner Larry Miller and I have seen repeated instances of this not only on his family's Michigan property but also on my own farm in southeastern Ohio where a panoramic view from several windows allows us to keep tabs on various meadows, cornfield perimeters, grown-over fields and forested edges. And it never ceases to amaze us how, when the weather turns sour for several days, it seems as if every deer in the county has suddenly vanished. Yet then, just as suddenly, when there is a dramatic change in the weather deer are everywhere.

Biologists generally agree that these abrupt turnarounds in deer behavior are due to the effects of frontal conditions and related barometric changes that accompany them. By definition, a front is a line on a weather map that indicates the leading edge of a mass of predominantly cooler or warmer air advancing into some other region presently occupied by a markedly different air temperature. If the advancing weather system is a low-pressure front, a mass of colder air is destined to collide with warmer air, giving birth to sometimes extremely turbulent conditions characterized by high winds, rapidly dropping temperatures and precipitation in the form of rain, sleet or snow. Yet if the advancing weather is a high-pressure system, conditions generally begin moderating, although at the leading edge of that front there may be several days of rain or snow. To make the matter all the more confusing, high-pressure weather systems see winds consistently blowing in a clockwise direction, low-pressure systems consistently blow counterclockwise, yet both may temporarily reverse themselves when confronting land barriers such as mountain ranges. All of this is exactly why weather forecasting is such a short-term and often imprecise science.

What does all this mean to the deer hunter? Well, the vitally important thing to keep in mind about frontal systems is that a rapidly falling barometric pressure precedes the arrival of stormy, often violent weather. The moment that stormy weather arrives, there will be a sharp curtailment in deer activity. Until that time, hunt long and hard because deer, sensing the arrival of foul weather, will be out in full force stocking up on groceries. Days later, a low barometer that is beginning to rise is another invaluable signal. Soon the weather system will move through the region and deer will once again be out feeding.

## LOOK TO THE HEAVENS

If the evening sky at sunset is yellow, be prepared for strong winds the following day, especially during the midday period. Under these conditions, stillhunting or sitting on stand might produce deer sightings at the very crack of dawn, and then again during the final hour of dusk. Otherwise, I advise *not* hunting during the midday period from, say, 9 a.m. to 5 p.m., because deer will be holed-up in thick cover. If you try to penetrate such strongholds, you'll just catch a glimpse of white flags disappearing in the distance. This sensitizes the animals to the fact that they are being hunted and makes them far more cautious and wary. Big bucks may even move entirely out of the region to safer parts elsewhere or become almost exclusively nocturnal in their activities. Therefore, good advice is to spend the midday hours doing something other than hunting, such as studying maps and aerial photos, performing maintenance on equipment, or target shooting.

On the other hand, if the evening sky is red, it's an indication the following day should be calm and sunny. Now is when you want to forget about everything else and spend as much time afield as possible because deer may be up and around at any hour. Moreover, when individual deer do choose to bed, they won't hide in such thick cover that they will be unapproachable. If the weather is cold, they may even lie in the open on south-facing slopes.

Cloud formations can also tell an astute hunter what to expect in the way of impending weather and predictable deer behavior. In fact, I recommend visiting a bookstore and buying a little pocket manual describing cloud formations and related weather conditions they are associated with and keeping it in hunting camp. Here are a few of the more common examples that, when recognized, may help you get your buck.

When altocumulus clouds are gathering on the north or northwest horizon, and winds are coming from the south or southwest, it's a certainty the barometric pressure is falling and a frontal system is rapidly approaching. Pack a lunch, hunt pre-scouted feeding areas, and don't even think about returning to camp until dark.

You'll have no trouble recognizing the actual arrival of the frontal system. The altocumulus clouds you were observing will have grown steadily darker. Or they will have been quickly pushed through your region and been replaced by altostratus clouds which give the sky a solid, gunmetal gray overcast. The wind velocity, still coming from a southerly direction, will have increased dramatically and may, or may not, be accompanied by driving spits of rain or sleet, but it doesn't make any difference because the wind itself will have curtailed all deer activity.

Usually within a day or two, the frontal system will either begin dissipating or will have entirely pushed through your region. Once again, the sky tells the story. A clear, starlit night accompanied by a gentle breeze from the north or northwest should tell you to hit the sack early because tomorrow will be splendid for all-day hunting. When you awaken in the morning, you'll undoubtedly notice very high and scattered cumulus clouds, which look like puffy globs of cotton. These conditions indicate the approach of a high-pressure system, moderating conditions and fair weather. But if they are absent, and there is a halo or corona around the moon, expect still another low-pressure frontal system. The halo is the result of moonlight shining through cirrostratus clouds that are the forerunners of unsettled weather destined to arrive within forty-eight hours.

Similarly, if the sky remains a solid leaden gray, with swiftly moving nimbostratus clouds, and the wind continues to come from a southerly direction, be prepared for several more days of foul weather.

Lower cirrus clouds—known as mare's tails—also foretell bad weather, usually in the form of snow. Cumulonimbus clouds, with a base several miles wide and an anvil-shaped top that can reach 55,000 feet in height, predict severe thunderstorms.

**Altocumulus clouds give advance warning of the arrival of a frontal system, meaning that deer activity should sharply increase in several hours.**

When the frontal system arrives with its gunmetal gray altostratus clouds, wind velocity will dramatically increase and deer activity will cease. The front may be accompanied by rain or sleet.

Cumulus clouds herald the arrival of moderating conditions and fair weather.

This halo, or corona, effect around the moon is due to moonlight shining through cirrostratus clouds, meaning another foul-weather front is scheduled to arrive.

Nimbostratus clouds moving rapidly through a region also bring bad weather, usually in the form of snow.

Easily identified mare's tails (cirrus clouds) predict the arrival of snow.

Cumulonimbus clouds signal the arrival of severe thunderstorms. But until the wind and rain actually begin, deer activity should be intense.

## SEVERE WEATHER

Many hunters believe that in cold or inclement weather deer seek protection from the elements in order to be more comfortable. Actually, this is far from the truth. Scientists explain that a deer's brain is relatively small in relation to its overall body size. Therefore, the integrated nervous system coursing throughout its body is rudimentary at best. As a result, like most wild creatures that do not possess a sophisticated neural apparatus, a deer's pain threshold is quite high, making it relatively insensitive to bitter-cold temperatures. This is exactly why a deer can stand barefooted in the snow for weeks on end, whereas it would be very painful for a human to do so for just a few minutes. Why, then, do deer frequently elect to bed on sun-drenched slopes in bitter-cold weather? It's because they instinctively know to conserve body energy at a time of year when food supplies are the least plentiful.

Consequently, "bodily comfort" has little to do with the changed behavior patterns deer often exhibit in the face of harsh weather conditions. After all, the northern boundary of the whitetail's native range extends more than 150 miles beyond the U.S./Canadian border to approximately 52 degrees latitude. And anyone

**Bitter-cold weather doesn't bother whitetails, but it does govern much of their behavior.**

who has lived thereabouts can tell you that winter temperatures frequently *average* -20 degrees. The wind-chill factor often makes it seem as cold as -75 degrees. It just doesn't stand to reason that whitetails would be native to such hostile climes were they not virtually immune to such weather.

I've described this aspect of whitetail physiology for good reason. In severe weather, when it seems as if the animals have evaporated, don't look for deer in places where they can be warmer, drier, or otherwise more comfortable. Instead, try to find security cover that allows the animals the most efficient use of their senses. And, as often as not, this may be a place you consider entirely unfavorable.

A clear example of this occurred just last year when I was hunting whitetails in Georgia with my friend Bill Jordan, the designer of the famous RealTree camouflage pattern. It was not cold, but driving rainstorms day after day hampered our hunting. Nevertheless, we had no trouble finding deer and eventually filled our tags.

The terrain just south of Atlanta is gently rolling to mountainous. We sought thick stands of conifers located on steep, sloping hillsides and then stillhunted along the downwind edges. You might think that deer in the vicinity would be buried deeply in the thick pines to shelter themselves from the pounding rain, but this wasn't the case. They didn't care at all about getting wet. Rather, they were along the edge of

**During periods of inclement weather, look for deer against the protected lee side of heavy cover that walls out the drone of the wind.**

the pines, in the open, where the wind would carry any sound or smell of danger from within the forest. From there they could look downslope through the open hardwoods below them. By slowly poking along the edge of the pines, we were able to sneak to within forty yards of bedded deer and loose our arrows.

## LET THE WIND WORK FOR YOU

The wind is always a deer's best friend or worst enemy. For hunters, too little wind is just as bad as too much.

A moderating, prevailing wind, meaning less than twelve miles an hour and consistently coming from the same direction, is a deer's ally. When the wind is above twelve miles an hour, deer hunker down and will not move unless they are almost stepped on, and even then they may run just a short distance before ducking down again. Conversely, if the air is dead calm, deer are likely to be moving, but they'll be easily alerted by even the slightest body movement on your part; even a barely audible sound such as a whisker stubble grating on your jacket collar as you turn your head may send deer hightailing for the boondocks.

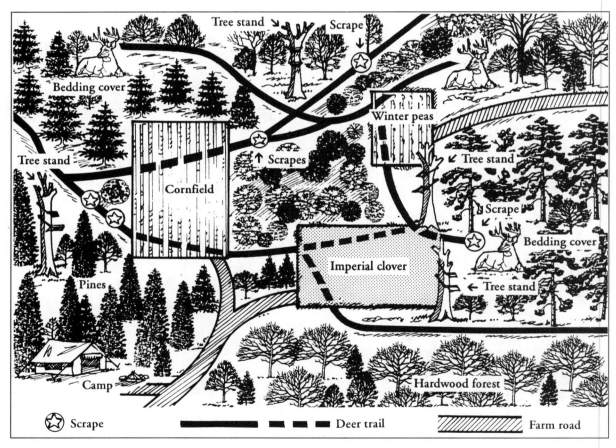

Don't burn out stands by repeated use and don't use stands when the wind is not in their favor. In this hypothetical sketch showing feeding areas, bedding areas, deer trails and tree stands, consider how changing wind directions from one day to the next would determine which stand you'd elect to use and how you'd approach it.

I like a slight amount of wind. A gentle breeze of five miles an hour is perfect. This causes vegetation to sway ever so gently, and dry leaves to barely rustle, both of which help to camouflage any sounds or movements I make, yet such soft winds are not at all unsettling to deer.

Perhaps the most defeating conditions are erratic, swirling breezes that seem to buffet you from every direction at once, or entirely reverse themselves from one minute to the next. I try to avoid hunting under these conditions because there is no way to control the direction my scent is blowing. And when it is blowing in every direction at once, deer are sure to detect my presence.

In fact, now's a good time to use *several* stands. After you've invested plenty of time scouting the terrain, pegging the routine of various animals, and establishing a terrific stand, it just doesn't make sense to use that stand too frequently or when conditions aren't just right. Deer will become alert to your movements and you'll burn out the stand.

From past experience I've learned it's not wise to hunt from the same stand more than two consecutive days. Give it a rest while you occupy another stand elsewhere. Keep the deer guessing so they never know where you are. Moreover, never hunt a given stand when the wind has done a turnaround and it is no longer in your favor at that stand location. I even make the effort never to use the same exact route to travel to and from a stand each time I use it. Vary your approach from slightly different directions whenever possible.

## THE NEMESIS OF SNOW

Snow is yet another potential deterrent to successful deer hunting, and it can thwart the best laid plans when it comes in sudden, large amounts. As noted earlier, the temperature drop accompanying snowfall does not make deer cold and uncomfortable. Rather, it is the marked change heavy snow has on their environment that unnerves them. There no longer are the same smells and sights that were so familiar just the day before, and it often takes twenty-four hours *after* the snow for them to calm down, leave their beds and resume normal activities. So if you wake one morning and discover driving snowflakes pinging against your windowpane and rapidly accumulating on the ground, sitting on stand is likely to be futile.

# 15

# Stand and Blind Setups

## TREE STANDS

If you were to poll a cross-section of deer hunters who use tree stands and ask them the most important factor in the success or failure of a hunt, the majority would probably name stand placement.

For bowhunters this is especially important, for they must set up within whispering distance of where they intend to arrow their quarry. And when the shooting distance is so close that they can see vapor coming from a buck's nostrils and count the bumps on his antler burrs, nothing can be left to chance.

The gun hunter must likewise engineer his tree stand setup with great care. While it is true that a hunter armed with a scoped rifle can reach out as far as 300 yards and even beyond, many of the largest bucks recorded by gun hunters every year are taken within spitting distance.

Most authorities concede that the ideal shooting range for bowhunting is somewhere between ten to twenty yards. Even though you may be capable of placing arrows accurately at thirty-five yards or beyond, it's not wise to shoot this far when deer hunting due to a deer's ability to dodge the flight of the arrow.

Some hunters are reluctant to accept this fact, believing that arrows travel so fast, especially from modern compound bows, that it's virtually impossible for deer to jump the string, but this is a misconception.

It is not the sight of an arrow that deer react to but the sound of the string being released. Even if you use a string silencer, your string will still make a slight twang, which can cause a deer to instinctively duck.

The fastest compound bows on the market generally chronograph at less than 230 feet per second. Sound travels at 1,088 feet per second. Therefore, any noise you make will reach the deer *five times faster* than your arrow.

Since it takes a deer only three-tenths of a second to drop a full body size, and since at twenty-five yards it takes your arrow at least five-tenths of a second to reach its target, it's clear why many bowhunters score clean misses. But at eighteen yards or less, it takes an arrow only two-tenths of a second to reach its target, giving the deer no time to duck before it arrives.

Obviously, most of us would probably be tempted to take a shot at a big buck beyond twenty-five yards. But if you place your stand within twenty yards of where you expect to see a deer, you'll have fewer misses. If an occasional twenty-five-yard shot does present itself, and you can't resist taking it, remember to aim low—in the vicinity of the heart—so that when the animal ducks the arrow will hit the lung region.

Next to distance, position in relation to the sun is an important consideration in stand placement. Once on a hunt in North Carolina, I was sitting on what I thought was an ideal stand near a trail hub. As late afternoon approached and the sun began sinking to the skyline, it became increasingly more difficult to see the trail. Then, just when the sun had become almost blinding, an impressive ten-pointer appeared. By this time my burning eyes were squinted almost closed and stinging tears were streaming down my face. I raised my arm in slow motion to wipe my eyes with my jacket sleeve, but apparently the deer caught the slight movement and quickly evaporated into the bright haze.

The lesson learned from this experience is that, aside from the difficulty of looking directly into the sun, bright sunlight tends to magnify even the smallest movement.

To reverse this situation, if you're an early-morning hunter, position your tree stand so that the rising sun in the east is on your back and its bright rays are slanting in the direction you expect deer to approach. If you're an evening hunter, you'll want your back to the west to achieve the same end. If you hunt both mornings and evenings, you'll of course need two stands in different places.

It's possible to situate a stand with the sun at your back and still be bathed in bright light by being too exposed. It's important to take a stand within cover where long tentacles of shadows will help to break up your outline. Some hunters like to have heavy brush, vegetation or tree branches immediately behind them. Even better is being partly encircled by cover.

Most accomplished hunters study specific tree species that may best suit their needs. The late-winter/early-spring period is an ideal time for this owing to the lack of foliage.

As an example of how important this is, I'm reminded of many years ago when I still did all of my scouting just prior to opening day. One season I had chosen a maple tree which had plenty of leaves clustered about fifteen feet off the ground, and that's where I hung my portable stand. The leaves had long since lost their brilliant fall colors and had turned brown, but they nevertheless offered adequate concealment.

One day I was sitting in my stand when brisk winds began buffeting the region. As the storm front approached closer and closer, leaves began blowing everywhere, and in less than two hours the maple had shed every bit of its foliage, leaving me completely exposed.

So keep in mind that early in the season, when autumn foliage still is present, virtually any type of leafy tree may be suitable. But consider what the tree will look like in weeks to come.

Although many species become so denuded that not even a sparrow could find hiding, exceptions of course are the various evergreens (pines, firs, spruces, cedars) which retain their bushy boughs year-round to afford excellent concealment. I also favor oak trees. Even though an oak's leaves will eventually turn brown and die, they remain securely affixed to their stem attachments long into the dead of winter. The same is true of yellow and tulip poplar, beech and certain hickory species.

Another important feature of a tree stand is moderately thick ground vegetation along the trail edges. The cover should be dense enough almost to conceal an approaching deer, to give you time to prepare for the shot.

Each year many hunters can be seen trudging into the woods carrying portable stands with bright, unpainted wooden and aluminum frame

Although this hunter is dressed in full camo, he has chosen the wrong tree. With the leaf-drop now complete, he is now fully exposed and a deer will catch his slightest movement.

If you cannot find a tree that retains its leaves well into the dead of winter, pick a tree with many gnarled branches and forked limbs to break up your outline.

Evergreens retain their leafy boughs year-round to afford ideal concealment.

members that virtually doom their hunt from the beginning.

When you buy a stand, the first thing to do is spray all exposed surfaces with flat black paint. Then, with light green or olive-drab paint, break up the stand's appearance with vertical bars and stripes. Although not as critical to the gun hunter as the bowhunter, I like to paint my stand with a product known as U.V. Shield to eliminate any reflective glow from the paint and even attach several camo leaf strips to the stand's struts and frame members.

Today veteran hunters aren't climbing as high as they did in previous years. The only time a high stand is advantageous is when you're in a tree which does not have assorted limbs and leafy branches to break up your outline or when you're hunting on a steep mountainside and the deer are expected to approach from an uphill direction. Then and only then is it necessary to be twenty or even twenty-five feet off the ground to be out of a deer's plane of vision.

Just keep in mind, when bowhunting, that the acute downward angle of the shot increases proportionately with a tree stand's height. In many instances, a portable stand hung no more

**Never use a new tree stand without first spray-painting it to cover all bright, shiny surfaces.**

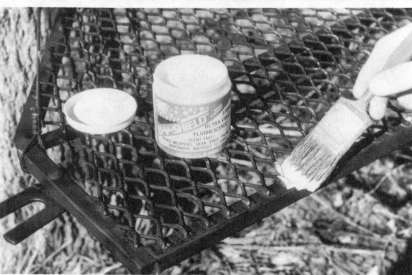

**Many paints contain ultraviolet pigments that will alert deer to your presence. After spray-painting your stand, treat it with U.V. Shield.**

than six feet off the ground may be perfectly acceptable if the tree has many gnarled, disfigured limbs and leafy branches at that level to conceal you.

If you've found an ideal tree for your stand but there is little cover at a desirable height, one possibility is attaching cover gathered from nearby. But don't begin indiscriminately cutting cover from the vicinity surrounding your stand or you'll eliminate the screens described earlier which are needed to block an approaching deer's line of vision. Instead gather the cuttings pruned from the shooting alleys leading to your stand. Next, depending upon the location of existing branches in the tree of your choice, use a folding saw to reduce your shooting alley cut-

tings to straight sapling sections and leafy crown sections. The straight sapling sections can then be tied horizontally in place and the leafy crown sections inverted so they hang upside-down by branch crotches from the horizontals. In just a few minutes, your stand will be almost completely melted into your surroundings.

## GROUND BLINDS

Sometimes you may conclude that a tree stand is unnecessary and that a ground blind would be a better form of concealment. In fact, one or two ground blinds can save the day when high winds, driving sleet and plummeting air temperatures make climbing into a tree stand foolhardy.

If there is little cover at the stand level, attach sapling cross-members and hang inverted leafy branches removed from your shooting lanes.

This hunter has done an excellent job of using branch cuttings to completely conceal his stand and the lower half of his body.

Here a drape of camo cloth provides a ground blind. It adequately conceals the hunter, but a deer may spot him when he rises to shoot.

Many hunters tack or staple a length of camo cloth between two saplings, or pile up brush, and then merely hide behind it. This may suffice for a rifleman watching a trail crossing or feeding area 100 yards away. But if a buck unexpectedly slips in from behind, you may blow your shooting opportunity.

Similarly, this particular type of blind construction is unsuited for bowhunting. Inevitably you'll want to peer over the top edge of the blind to watch for deer traffic, exposing your head and shoulders. Then, when the moment of truth arrives, you have to rise still higher to draw your bow, which exposes still more of your upper body, and your movements may frighten the deer.

Cover placed *behind* you and *overhead* is just as important, maybe even more so, than cover placed in front of you. The obvious reason, of course, is that thick screening cover entirely surrounding your position completely hides you from view from all directions. The word "blind" may even be somewhat of a misnomer because the finished creation should actually resemble an igloo.

## Portable Blinds

Although most hunters prefer to build their own blinds from a combination of native cover and other materials, there are numerous portable deer blinds on the market. To my knowledge all are lightweight, and since they pop up into shape by means of internal wands, they can be erected in minutes. Their main disadvantage is their cost, with better quality models fetching $80 to $200. Just one example of a quality blind is the Hide-Out (P.O. Box 1801, Elkhart, IN 46515).

As easily portable as these blinds are, they are most effective when left in one place for long periods of time so that local deer become

An alternative to a hand-crafted blind is a commercially made, portable model that can be left in place for some time.

entirely accustomed to seeing them. Also, check the sizes of the zippered windows; if you're a bowhunter, you'll want windows in the form of long, vertical rectangles.

## Constructing a Blind

Like tree stands, no two ground blinds ever look alike, but a few building tips will go a long way toward ensuring that you remain as inconspicuous as possible.

An unobtrusive blind is one that as closely as possible matches the height of surrounding native cover. If the ground cover is low and sparse, and the dome of the blind is to match that cover height, it may be necessary to dig a shallow pit for you to sit on a stool. For a gun hunter, the pit can be circular in shape, but a bowhunter requires a diamond-shaped pit to enable him to draw his bow in frontal, right and left directions.

If possible, I like to gather brush and branches and, using twine or lightweight wire to hold them in place where necessary, build an

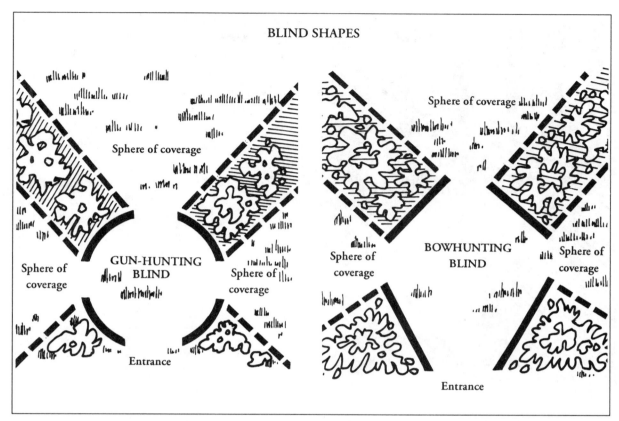

**BLIND SHAPES**

A gun hunter's blind can be circular in shape, with three shooting windows. But a bowhunter's blind must be diamond-shaped to allow for raising and drawing his bow.

igloo-like structure. With pruning shears I cut three small openings to shoot through. These can be 10-inch-diameter holes for a gun, but they should be 6-by-20-inch-tall vertical slots for a bow.

Another option is to poke a number of upright sticks into the ground to encircle the blind site and then staple camo cloth in place. Lately I've been using Hide-um-Hunter cloth (Brell Mar Products, 5701 Hwy 80 W, Jackson, MS 39209). This is a premium-quality blind material available in every major camo pattern presently on the market, so it can be adapted to different types of terrain.

In using any form of camo cloth, remember to fabricate a roof by laying the cloth over cross-hatched branches tied overhead. Then place additional leafy branches or other native cover around the circumference of the structure to further break up the appearance of the blind.

Naturally, you'll have to fashion some means of entering and exiting your little abode. I suggest a small crawlway that you have to enter on hands and knees, situated on the downwind, backside of the blind because this is the least likely direction from which a deer may approach.

The next step, which is a little-known secret of effective blind construction, is to use several square yards of black tarpaper or dark-colored cloth to line the inside ceiling and back wall. Simply tuck it in place behind branch stubs and wire or tie it elsewhere as necessary.

The tarpaper or black cloth accomplishes two things. First, that portion affixed to the ceiling

Seat

substantially darkens the inside of the hut so that, from the outside, it's very difficult to ascertain slight movements within. Equally important, the backdrop prevents you from being silhouetted against the otherwise light-colored background if the sun is behind you.

The last step is to put something inside to sit on. In most instances, a folding campstool will suffice. But if it's a pit blind, a still better idea, when digging the hole, is to fashion a bucket seat in the earth at the rear of the blind. With a boat cushion to sit on, and a backrest to lean against, the seat is just as comfortable as an easy chair.

**If it's necessary to dig a pit blind, use a shovel to cut a seat and backrest into the soil.**

# 16

# Failsafe Stand and Blind Locations

Unquestionably one of the greatest challenges a deer hunter faces is determining exactly where to wait in hiding for his quarry. This is difficult because of the many factors that influence the behavior of whitetails.

For example, weather has a dramatic impact upon deer, causing them to do entirely different things, in different places, on clear days than on days when they are assaulted by heavy rains or driving winds. The rutting period likewise causes deer to sharply deviate in their travels, as do the changing diets of the animals as the season progresses. Even hunting pressure, which may range from nonexistent in some places to intense in others, can make stand or blind placement critically important.

The hunter who selects just one stand or blind location for use throughout the entire season is short-changing himself. He needs to be flexible and choose his spot carefully based on the above conditions, knowing full well that tomorrow he may have to occupy an alternate stand or blind located elsewhere.

Following are eighteen different types of loca-

tions where a hunter could situate a stand or blind with high expectations of taking a deer.

## MAJOR DEER RUNWAYS

Major deer runways serve as travel corridors between bedding and feeding areas. While a network of other threadlike trails may crisscross the terrain, there is no mistaking a major runway. It may be quite wide, due to generations of deer repeatedly using this thoroughfare, and the soil will have become so compacted over the years that little vegetation grows there. Although a major deer runway may course through a tract of forestland, you're more likely to find it in conjunction with restrictive terrain features such as long, narrow hollows, lengthy streambottoms, or where different types of tree species meet (such as pines bordering hardwoods).

Throughout the fall and winter months, major deer runways are predominantly used by doe-family groups (one or two does, their most recent offspring and perhaps a spike buck,

Major deer runways become so compacted through continual use that they are easy to identify. They are used mostly by does, except during the peak of the rut when bucks follow females approaching estrus.

forkhorn or daughter from the previous season). Mature bucks use major deer runways only during the peak-rut phase of the mating period when they are engaging in trail transference in order to follow does approaching the height of their estrous cycles.

## SECONDARY DEER TRAILS

Secondary deer trails are used by mature bucks during the non-rutting weeks of early fall and late winter. Mature bucks do not like to associate with doe-family units at this time, preferring to keep their private lives private. Occasionally, you may find a secondary deer trail paralleling a major deer runway on the runway's downwind side and in much heavier cover; this allows a buck to keep tabs on the activities of other deer and even to use them as sentries to forewarn him of danger.

However, in a majority of cases, mature bucks will adopt their own home ranges away from doe-family groups. Secondary deer trails can be difficult to identify because they are not tamped down to the same degree as major deer runways and this allows vegetation to hide them from view in many places.

A very light skiff of snow on the ground makes the task of identifying such trails infinitely easier. Be especially alert for the absence of very small tracks. When small tracks are found in conjunction with large tracks, a doe-family unit is using the trail, not a lone buck.

Secondary deer trails are usually downwind of major deer runways and are difficult to identify because they are not tamped down.

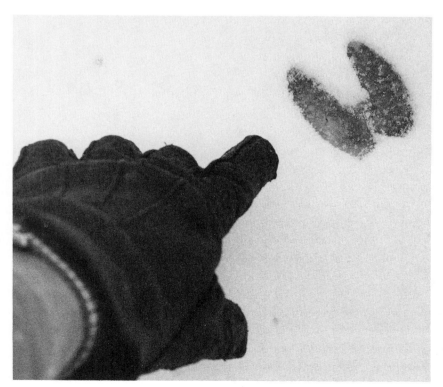

Post-season scouting is best way to find secondary deer trails used by bucks. A light blanket of snow on the ground makes track analysis easy.

## SCRAPE CLUSTERS

A mature whitetail buck may create as many as three-dozen scrapes during the pre-rutting period, but a majority of them are quickly abandoned, and only a very few become elevated in status to primary scrapes. Moreover, situating a stand in the vicinity of clusters of scrapes is generally far more productive than merely standing watch over a single primary, because the concentrated nature of the breeding sign indicates the animal's revisitation on a far more frequent basis.

What most hunters do not understand about the rutting period is that waiting on a stand near primary scrapes is most effective only during the pre-breeding phase of the rut (about two weeks before does reach the zenith of their estrous cycles). During the peak of the rut, scrape hunting continues to be effective, but a much wiser tactic is to occupy a stand overlooking a major deer runway or a doe-family bedding area because anxious bucks will be spending less time tending their scrapes and increasingly more time in the vicinity of does, waiting for the very first ones to become receptive.

It's worth mentioning that ideal scrape locations are always at a premium and thereby see use by successive generations of mature bucks. If you kill a buck near a concentration of primary scrapes, scout the same ground the following year and you'll undoubtedly discover another mature buck has meanwhile moved in to occupy the area and is likewise making scrapes in the same immediate vicinity.

## TRAIL HUBS

A trail hub is where two or more trails cross. Intersecting major deer runways always have the

Lakeshores and other natural barriers tend to contain deer activity and thus reveal the presence of perimeter trails.

most deer traffic (in the form of does, their current offspring and immature bucks). Intersecting secondary deer trails have less traffic; since virtually all of the animals will be mature bucks, these are the best places to locate a stand during the non-rutting period.

As the rut intensifies, look for a trail hub where a secondary deer trail (buck trail) intersects with a major deer runway being used by doe-family groups. Usually you'll see plenty of different-aged animals passing by.

Several years ago, in Potter County, Pennsylvania, I located a major deer runway intersected by *two* secondary trails and was astounded at the continual deer traffic. I had only two days to bowhunt, during which a total of thirty-seven deer passed my stand, including five mature bucks.

Keep in mind that the greatest incidence of trail hubs occurs on relatively level terrain where the cover is of mixed species. It is rare to find trail hubs in steep mountain terrain because deer usually follow terrain contours.

## PERIMETER TRAILS

A whitetail's home range averages less than two square miles and the outer perimeter is quite often delineated by major terrain features. Examples include lakeshores, rivercourses, sheer rocky bluffs, deep gorges, and forest edges which yield to prairieland.

Scout these likely home-range boundary areas and you'll find trails. When deer are engaging in routine daily behavior, perimeter trails are infrequently used. But if there are few does in the region and the rut is in progress, bucks will patrol their boundary areas, covering many

**Trail hubs provide exciting action because of the sheer numbers of animals a hunter sees each day.**

miles per day in search of estrous females. Similarly, if hunting pressure mounts, bucks will filter out of their usual haunts to find seclusion in peripheral areas, whereupon perimeter trails suddenly may become hotspots worth watching. Yet sometimes just the opposite occurs and intense hunting pressure causes bucks to retreat to the innermost sanctuaries of their core areas where they cling tenaciously to their beds and don't even blink.

## ESCAPE TRAILS

Under intense hunting pressure, and especially when hunters are engaged in making drives, deer immediately vacate their areas of normal activity and head for very heavy cover or difficult terrain. Knowing this, and knowing in advance where that hunting pressure is likely to originate, watching an escape trail can pay handsome dividends.

Begin by using maps to drive all main and secondary roads in the immediate area you plan to hunt. Look for campgrounds where you can be sure other hunters will establish week-long bases of operation during deer season. Also look for trailheads or wide places along the berm where day hunters are likely to park and enter the woodlands.

Next, locate the most nightmarish cover you can find in the region. It might be a swamp, or a spruce bog, but it could also be a ravine

Learn to dope out the activities of other hunters in your region and where hunting pressure will originate. Then find the nearest, heaviest escape cover and be there to intercept deer when other hunters arrive on opening day.

Deer will not hesitate to cross rivers to safety of islands or the opposite shore. Look for tracks in the shoreline mud to find a good ambush point.

choked with brush and jackstrawed logs, a pine plantation, or a jungle of tall vegetation such as rhododendron. Then search for tracks entering the cover. If you can find tracks that are splayed and eight to ten feet apart, indicating a bounding animal, you've found an escape trail.

Then select a stand location between the place where hunter pressure will predictably originate and the heaviest nearby escape cover. If the stars are in your favor, this pressure will push plenty of deer past your stand on opening day, almost as if the other hunters were acting as drivers.

One of the most overlooked escape havens used by deer is an island in mid-river. Deer will not hesitate to swim a river anymore than you'd hesitate to cross a street. The sure tip-off that deer are hiding on an island is evidence of tracks in the shoreline mud of the riverbank which suddenly disappear into the water, especially if

there is a shallow riffle or gravel bar. Again, if you can peg a hunter-pressure point nearby, chances are the place where you have determined deer are entering the water can be worth its weight in venison.

## RUB-LINE TRAILS

Essentially, a rub line indicates a secondary deer trail used by a buck. But compared to a secondary trail used by a buck on a year-round basis, a rub-line trail is used most frequently during the pre-rut period. The main purpose of the trail is to provide a travel route between bedding and feeding areas. But if it's within the area where the buck hopes to breed, he marks it with visual and olfactory signposts. As the rut gets fully underway, a rub-line trail may also connect scrapes strung out across the countryside.

A recent rub will reveal a moist, light-colored cambium, while one which is weeks old will have begun to dry and turn slightly gray. I like to find rub lines in which there are individual rubs that are very fresh, moderately old and very old, as this indicates the animal is traveling that specific route on a regular basis, making it an ideal location for stand placement. Moreover, if you can find a rub-line trail where many of the individual rubs are scarred and healed over, it's a sure indication the trail is heavily used every year by subsequent generations of bucks.

## DOE-FAMILY BEDDING AREAS

Does and their most recent offspring generally bed in thickets or midway up sloping terrain, as opposed to bottomlands or along ridges. To identify major deer runways used by doe-family groups, look for large and small tracks and large and small matted ovals in the ground. You should also see large and small droppings.

The prime time to hunt a doe-family bedding area is the pre-breeding phase of the rut, as amorous bucks will be nearby anxiously waiting for the first does to enter estrus. A stand should be located some distance (at least 100 yards) from the actual bedding area, on a major deer runway leading toward it, to avoid getting too close and alerting the animals to your presence. This is vitally important because if the does feel their security has been violated and decide to leave the area, any bucks in the immediate vicinity are sure to follow them.

## MATURE-BUCK BEDDING AREAS

Mature bucks generally bed higher than doe-family units and in thicker cover. Since mature bucks are usually solitary animals, look for a

**Doe-family bedding areas are usually located midway up sloping terrain, and the prime time to hunt them is just before the rut begins.**

lone bed in a region pockmarked with numerous rubs on saplings, and a combination of old and fresh tracks and droppings.

There are three best times to wait on a stand near a mature-buck bedding area. The first is very early in the season, well before the pre-breeding period of the rut. The second is after the rut is concluded and exhausted bucks enter the recuperative phase of the season and thus spend more time than usual in their bedding areas. The third is any time the immediate area is subjected to intense hunting pressure.

A mature buck's selection of a bedding area is based solely upon the feeling of safety offered by that place. If you violate the buck's security by installing your stand too close, he'll vacate the region and begin bedding elsewhere. I advise setting up at least 200 yards away from a mature buck's bedding area, on a secondary deer trail leading from the bedding region to a prime food source, and occupying your stand only on those days when the wind is absolutely in your favor.

## GRAZING AREAS

Early in the season, before killer frosts wipe out lush vegetation, whitetails are primarily grazers. Search for secluded grassy openings, hay meadows, soybean fields and native species of greenery which deer in that region prefer. Then establish a stand that will allow you to watch the food site at morning's first light and again at dusk.

South of the Mason-Dixon line, the vegetation found in typical grazing areas may remain green throughout the winter. However, most species turn woody or stemmy and no longer are succulent and palatable. The one exception to this, as described in Chapter 7, is ladino clover blends such as Imperial Whitetail Clover, which are now being extensively planted in many regions. These clover blends are likewise beginning to appear in scattered locations throughout the North as well, and they can be deer magnets

after hard frosts have caused other vegetation to turn brown and fall into a dormant state.

## BROWSING AREAS

As the season progresses and all vegetation except ladino clover blends begin turning brown and entering a dormant state, whitetails become browsers and now dote upon the tender twigs, buds and branch tips of regenerative saplings and immature brush. No matter where you live within the whitetail's range, you should be able to find either white cedar, red maple, mountain maple or black ash. Remember, the browse material must be within their reach, and this means finding immature trees with branches close to the ground.

As each month passes, deer gradually adjust their feeding periods toward the midday hours. Early in the season, of course, dawn and dusk are prime times to encounter deer en route to and from prime food sources, but during December and January their peak feeding time is generally from 10 a.m. to 3 p.m. Now is the time of year when they spend the cooler morning and night hours in their beds resting and conserving energy.

## ICE-CREAM FOODS

In every region of the country, local deer prefer certain foods. Since these foods generally are available for only very brief periods, they draw animals from afar.

Examples of these ice-cream foods include acorns, orchard fruits, and the crop-residue spillage of harvested corn, soybeans, carrots and sugarbeets. Imperial Brand Whitetail Clover blend is the only ice-cream food I know of that is available to deer year-round.

Occupy your stand early and late in the day, just prior to the arrival of a storm front or, best of all, immediately after several days of inclement weather.

Late in the season, after bitter-cold weather has killed vegetation, deer switch from grazing on ground vegetation to browsing on twigs. Nationwide, one of their favorite winter foods is white cedar.

## TRANSITION ZONES

Transition zones, which are sometimes referred to as staging areas, consist of 100- to 200-yard-wide bands of thick cover surrounding grazing areas, browsing areas or ice-cream food areas. If a given food site is relatively close to occupied dwellings or roads, deer will mill around in a transition zone until evening darkness sets in before exposing themselves in the open to feed. The same is also true in secluded regions where hunting pressure is intense.

Therefore, after finding one of the three types of feeding areas which deer are frequenting, scout the adjacent cover for approach trails and place your stand at least fifty yards back in the cover so that you'll be able to see your quarry before evening shooting light fades.

Morning stands in transition zones might have to be as much as 100 yards from the actual food site because mature bucks often leave the open feeding grounds before dawn's shooting light arrives. Getting into a morning stand can be tricky. If you cross the open meadow or other feeding area, you'll chase away deer feed-

An excellent example of transition-zone cover bordering a feeding area. Deer will usually remain back in a staging area of brush and immature trees and not step out until just before dark.

ing there. Much wiser is to circle the feeding area, come in from behind your stand or blind, and wait for the animals to conclude their feeding and begin drifting in your direction.

## DRINKING SITES

Under normal conditions, typical whitetail habitat has abundant "sheet water" in the form of streams, rivers, lakes and springs. But deer are opportunists and will also drink from rainwater puddles, stock tanks, farmponds and roadside ditches.

Consequently, drinking sites are *not* good places to establish stands under normal conditions when rainfall has been adequate enough to provide the animals with widespread drinking opportunities.

The prime time to sit on a stand near a source of water is during a severe drought in which all but the largest drinking sites are dry. Tracks peppering the area around a drinking site tell you how many animals are visiting it and their probable sexes.

The best time of day to occupy a stand near a known source of water is early morning after the deer have concluded their daybreak feeding. In the evening, deer do not customarily show up at a drinking site until after dark.

## CLEARCUTS AND BURNS

When a forest fire ravages the terrain, everything looks charred and horrible for many months. However, ash deposits reduce the pH content of the soil and what emerges is extremely succulent, high-quality regenerative vegetation that draws deer from surrounding areas.

Frequently check with your local Forest Service office to learn where clearcutting operations are underway, or where there has been a forest fire. In just two years, these places will regenerate lush food and attract deer.

When logging companies clearcut a tract of climax forestland, the elimination of the trees likewise scars the landscape. Yet with the overhead, shade-producing canopy now eliminated, a profusion of ground-story plants and saplings emerge, providing deer with a cornucopia of feeding opportunities.

Periodically check with your local Forest Service office to learn of recent forest fires or logging operations and you'll undoubtedly find more deer per square mile in those regions than elsewhere.

## STORMY-WEATHER BEDDING AREAS

Deer are relatively immune to the effects of precipitation, but when it occurs in conjunction with winds exceeding ten miles per hour they bed down in protective cover. Every hunter should have at least one stand overlooking a trail leading into or through a stormy-weather bedding area.

Because they retain their leaves year-round, conifers are the most favored stormy-weather bedding sites.

In the absence of evergreens, look for "walls." These are the protected lee sides of thick cover such as multiflora rose, honeysuckle or tag alders, or steep boulder-riddled terrain, all of which block the wind and allow deer to make maximum use of their senses.

## TERRAIN CHANNELS

A terrain channel is any natural or man-made terrain feature that funnels deer traffic in a certain direction. An example of a natural terrain channel might be a constricted bottleneck in steep bottomland that deer traffic must squeeze through in order to reach an adjacent region. A man-made terrain channel might be a permanently open gate in a fenceline or a place where the fence is broken, or even a shallow irrigation ditch that crosses an open field.

Also scout for narrow corridors through thick stands of cover or even blown-down trees which force deer to make a detour.

## CROSSING AREAS

Next time you see a precautionary "deer crossing" sign along the highway, pull over onto the berm and spend a few minutes studying your surroundings. Likely as not, you'll see that both sides of the road consist of long stretches of relatively open ground except for one specific place where two opposing tracts of woodland closely border the road. That is precisely where the sign has been placed.

Whitetails are cover-loving creatures, yet periodically they must cross fields and even highways during their travels. Naturally, they'll most often cross at a place where they are not exposed for any longer than necessary.

When scouting, try to find terrain which is similar to a highway deer crossing—that is, a piece of open ground where two opposing wooded points almost meet. When deer want to travel from one woodlot to the other, they'll probably cross near the wooded points.

A low saddle crossing a steep ridge can also be a hotspot. The dip in the contour of the terrain gives deer a sense of security.

Still another type of crossing I've found highly productive is a slightly elevated ridge of dry, wooded land separating two swamps.

Terrain channels cause deer to change their direction of travel. Here a buck skirts an area of blown-down trees.

Spooked deer will not hesitate to bound away through standing swamp water, but unalarmed animals going about their routine business will consistently prefer higher, drier ground.

## PICK OF THE LITTER

We've just described eighteen places which, given the right time of year and/or certain weather conditions, are surefire places to take a deer. Obviously, few of us would have the time to set up a stand in every place, but it would be unwise to prepare only one stand.

You should probably have three to five different stand sites every season. This will allow you to adapt to changing conditions and also to "rest" each of your stands now and then rather than burn out a single stand through continual use.

Of the eighteen stand locations described, it is imperative to have a stormy-weather stand. Otherwise, whenever severe weather strikes, you might as well just stay home because none of the other locations are likely to produce.

My second choice would be a trail hub, simply because part of the sheer fun and excitement of deer hunting is seeing lots of animals every day. By the same token, in being able to look over a number of different bucks, you stand a better chance of attaching your tag to an exceptional one.

A stand in a terrain channel area is essential if you live in a region where hunting pressure is light; if hunting pressure is intense, substitute an escape trail stand instead.

A stand overlooking a feeding area is a must. Make use of a portable stand in this location so you can switch from a grazing area to either a browsing area or specialty food area as the season progresses.

Finally, my fifth stand choice would be near a mature-buck bedding area, especially if a rub line, scrapes or large tracks suggest that the deer is a trophy animal.

# 17

# The Art of Stillhunting

As we've seen in previous chapters, whitetail deer live in unique social communities, establish hierarchal roles and communicate among each other.

The whitetail's foremost defenses are its eyes, nose and ears. If you can defeat any one of these senses, you should have no trouble sneaking to within rifle range. Defeat two of these senses and you may be able to arrow your buck. Defeat all three senses and you can reach right out and touch him!

For most hunters, the mere thought of getting so close to a deer as to be able to touch him might sound impossible. But it can be done, and Valerius Geist is a case in point. Serious students of whitetail behavior know Geist as one of the country's foremost deer biologists and, while students watch from afar, he repeatedly demonstrates his ability to touch deer.

We are certainly not suggesting here that if you heed the following advice you'll achieve the same results, nor should you even try. However, if you are able to get within thirty or forty yards of a deer, you should have an excellent chance of taking him with rifle or bow.

There are five essential elements in success-fully sneaking up on a buck. Botch any one of them and you'll alarm one or more of the deer's senses. You must hunt during the right times of day (there are two). You must hunt during the right type of weather. You must spot your trophy before it sees you. You must wear the most appropriate clothing. And you must make the right approach.

## TIME OF DAY

It is rather ironic that a majority of hunters usually elects to sit in a tree stand or ground-level blind during the early and late hours of the day and then stillhunt during the midday hours.

The reasoning these hunters use typically goes like this: "At dawn and dusk the animals are moving and so I'll let them come to me, but during midday they are usually bedded and so that's the time to go to them."

In reality, hunters should do just the opposite, for your very best chances of sneaking up on a buck are from dawn until about ten o'clock in the morning and then again from about four o'clock in the afternoon until dark.

**Stillhunting is best at dawn and dusk, not during midday.**

During the midday hours, when deer customarily are bedded, they are nearly impossible to approach. Bucks in particular select bedding locations which will afford them the utmost security and this gives them four distinct advantages. They are not moving but lying down and therefore difficult to see, and yet because of their cunningly chosen hideouts, they can easily see, hear or smell any predator. Thus your chances of slipping up on a bedded buck are only slightly better than winning your state's lottery.

Let's examine a stillhunting scenario as it might unravel during the early and late hours of the day and notice how everything dramatically turns around in your favor.

Early and late in the day your buck is probably on his feet, and this almost doubles the amount of his body exposed to view. He'll generally be in or around cover which is not nearly so dense and difficult to penetrate as the tangles where he beds, and this makes him even easier to see. Moreover, since he's on his feet, you can count on him to make some perceptible movements. But most important of all, when your buck is on his feet, he will be doing something. He may be feeding, or drinking, or thrashing his antlers against a sapling. Exactly what the animal is doing, however, really makes no difference, for it's the fact that he is engaged in some type of activity that swings the odds in your favor. During this activity, he usually pays little attention to what else may be going on in his immediate surroundings.

One time when stillhunting I spotted a six-point buck walking in my direction. His nose was tight to the ground and he was grunting, a sure indication he was trailing an estrous doe. I was caught in the open and froze, hoping my full camo attire would help me become a part of the forest's woodwork. As it happened, the wind was in my favor and the young buck, preoccupied with thoughts of courtship, came closer and closer.

When the deer passed me and was at a quar-

**Early and late in the day deer are generally on their feet and easier to see.**

When deer are on their feet, they usually are engaged in some type of activity and are oblivious to their surroundings.

tering-away angle, I drew my bow and shot him. I paced off the shooting distance; it was a scant twelve feet, the closest I've ever taken a whitetail. And the lesson learned has been ever-lasting: stillhunt early and late in the day when deer are on their feet.

## WEATHER

Some weather conditions are so poorly suited to stillhunting that the smartest thing you can do is stay home and clean out the garage. Don't try to stillhunt because you'll sensitize the animals to hunting pressure; they may go nocturnal and ruin your chances on succeeding days when conditions are perfect.

Strong winds should prompt you to stay home. Deer will remain bedded even during the early and late hours of the day when you'd otherwise expect them to be feeding. Conversely, no wind at all is just as bad, because when it is dead calm, it is impossible to move quietly.

A gentle, prevailing breeze is ideal. Deer will be on the move, but your own tiny noises will

be covered. By "prevailing," I mean that the breeze should be consistently moving in the same direction. If it's a non-prevailing breeze, in that it is erratic and swirling, your human scent will be carried in many unpredictable directions at once, warning deer of your presence. They may have difficulty pegging your exact location but that makes no difference, for simply catching a whiff of man odor is enough to make them leave the area.

Other conditions which make for ideal still-hunting include a soft rain, gentle snowfall or light fog. All enable you to walk silently. Yet an abrupt dive in the temperature will freeze the moisture-laden forest duff and other ground cover, and your feet will now crunch loudly.

### Study the Thermals

Related weather phenomena—thermal air currents—are more localized in nature. They travel up and down rather than horizontally like wind, and they are caused by changes in the air temperature.

Under stable weather conditions, thermal air currents drift downhill in the late evening and last through the early morning. "Downhill" also means down valleys, canyons and creek bottoms to lower elevations. Then, beginning sometime during the late morning, the thermals reverse themselves and head uphill to the crests of ridges and to the heads of hollows and draws.

Periods of unsettled weather are sure to affect the directional movement of thermal air currents. Rapidly clearing weather after a storm front sends the currents wafting to higher elevations, but a rapidly approaching frontal system, or one that already is in progress, causes them to cascade downhill.

When the topography is relatively flat, thermals drift out of heavy cover such as forests to more open places during the evening hours. This continues until early morning the following day. Then, about midmorning, there is a reversal, with the thermal drift from the open places toward heavy cover. Nevertheless, a prevailing wind exceeding five miles per hour will cancel out any thermal air currents.

With this knowledge, it's easy for a savvy hunter to better his chances of catching deer unaware. Deer, of course, continually monitor the wind for scent of approaching danger. But when there is little or no wind and the air seems perfectly still, they use thermals as their sentries.

You may have already noticed the effect of this without realizing what was happening. For

**Soft rain or snow makes for silent footing, but if the temperature rapidly begins to drop, the ground cover will begin to freeze and become crunchy.**

example, it's one reason why mature bucks head for higher ground to spend midday. They do it to have a good view of what's going on below but also because the typical upslope drift of the thermals during daylight hours will warn them well in advance of anything on the prowl. Conversely, most deer spend most of the night and dawn in the lower elevations as that is usually where food and water are most plentiful. But it's also because thermal air currents have now shifted and on lower ground the deer can more easily detect warning signals of danger approaching.

In flat country the same principle applies. Deer move into heavy cover in late morning and early afternoon, partly to hide and rest, but also because the thermals will be in their favor. In the evening and early morning, they are able to move into more open areas to feed and drink and yet still be on the alert.

When stillhunting, then, plan your movements so thermal air patterns are working in your favor instead of against you. Deer have tied their movements to the currents, and if you tailor your movements to them as well, you'll stand a far greater chance of seeing game. In hilly country, this means hunting upslope in the direction of bedding sites until no later than perhaps 10 a.m. Through the late morning, afternoon, and sometimes even into the very early evening, you must be on high ground such as ridges, hillside benches and canyon rims. In the flatlands, stay deep in the forests and heavy-cover regions during midday, and work the edges and clearings only during the evening or very early in the morning.

## CLOTHING

Many gun hunters don camouflage garments during the firearm season, but this can be very dangerous. Moreover, it's not really necessary because with a rifle in hand, a hunter is not required to get exceedingly close to deer. If you do decide to wear camo, wear a camo-orange vest treated with U.V. Killer so the upper part of your anatomy will be clearly visible to other hunters and yet not be overly conspicuous to deer.

On the other hand, it is imperative that bowhunters wear full camo because they have to get almost to within spitting range of their quarry. Many companies manufacture camo clothing, and I have found most of it to be of excellent quality.

However, most camo colors and design patterns are intended for specific situations, such as matching the bark of a hardwood tree or pine while you're sitting in an elevated stand, blending with cattails or cornstalks, and so on. But when stillhunting, you may find yourself near various types of tree cover as well as weedy vegetation, shrubs, brush and rocks. That's why I rely on RealTree's new All-Purpose pattern, which blends with the widest possible variety of terrain. RealTree camo is made by many different camo clothing manufacturers but is licensed by Spartan-Realtree Products, 1390 Box Circle Rd., Columbus, GA 31907.

Remember, too, that when bowhunting, it is vitally important to use total camo. This means giving due attention to your face and hands as well.

Since your feet play a crucial role in sneaking up on a buck, wearing the proper footwear can also spell the difference between success and failure. For many years I wore black tennis shoes because of the degree of sensitivity I achieved in feeling ground cover; alas, my feet were always cold and wet. Then I switched to boot-pacs; my feet stayed warm and dry but I sounded like a bull moose in a cornflake factory.

Happily, the Browning Company just introduced a new featherweight boot described as offering "stalking-foot comfort." These boots weigh only 22 ounces and contain Thinsulate, which has been found to be twice as warm as any other high-loft insulation, and Gore-Tex, which makes them 100 percent waterproof.

THE ART OF STILLHUNTING    177

## HOW TO SPOT DEER

It has been estimated that for every buck a hunter sees, at least four other bucks see him first and manage to slip away without his ever knowing of their presence. Undoubtedly this is because we view our environment in different ways.

Our eyes are situated in the front of our skull. This gives us keen binocular (two-eye) vision, while our lateral (side-to-side) vision is quite poor. Consequently, when we look off into the distance, we tend to focus upon a small area. If a deer is just a few yards outside of our concentrated area of focus, we probably won't see it, especially if the animal is standing still and is partly hidden by cover. Then you may think there are no deer around, begin your next step forward, and moments later see one or more white flags evaporating into the distance.

Deer, on the other hand, do not rely upon their binocular vision nearly as much as they do their wide-angle monocular vision, because it is the latter which allows them to catch the slightest of movements, especially around the periphery of their vision. It is only after a deer's attention is alerted by some movement that it relies on its binocular vision for identification and scrutiny.

When stillhunting, slowly scan the terrain from left to right, searching for the slightest movement. Then scan in the opposite direction, but ever more slowly, looking for a black nose, white throat patch or curved antler beam.

If you see nothing, don't move yet!

Next, study the ground at your feet to determine exactly where to place your advancing foot. Jackie Bushman, the founder of Buckmasters, in Montgomery, Alabama, has taken well over 150 splendid bucks, and he credits fancy footwork for many of them.

**Deer rely on their wide-angle monocular vision to scan their surroundings and pick up slight movements that may mean danger.**

"When taking each step forward, forget about your usual walking stride," Jackie advises, "because when you are negotiating cover and uneven terrain at a snail's pace, there is too much chance of falling off balance and inadvertently stepping on a dry twig. Take steps no longer than your boot size.

"Most hunters put their heel down first when taking a step, but this is a mistake because you've already committed your weight to that leading foot. If there is a brittle branch beneath that foot it will almost surely snap. Instead, place the ball of your foot down first because it is the eyes of your foot. It will feel the ground for you. Moreover, when you put the ball of your foot down first, you haven't transferred any weight to it. Once you feel solid footing, you can then lower your toe and heel and begin transferring your weight from the trailing foot to the lead foot. On the other hand, if you feel a branch begin to give beneath your foot, you can lift the foot and place it several inches away."

Paradoxically, if you do indeed accidentally snap a brittle twig or make a crunching noise upon dry leaves, the error doesn't automatically doom your efforts. The woodlands are actually very noisy places, and deer are accustomed to hearing turkeys and squirrels scuffling through the leaves, dead branches falling from overhead limbs and assorted other sounds. But the key is understanding that deer also have relatively brief attention spans, which biologists estimate to be less than three minutes. So when you make a noise, remember to freeze in place for at least several minutes. Your initial sound will have undoubtedly alerted any nearby deer, but if there are no other sounds from your direction they'll return to feeding or other activities, allowing you to advance another few steps before coming to a halt and once again searching the cover ahead from a slightly different perspective.

I'd also like to suggest an effective trick I've been using for several years to wend my way through nightmarish tangles with a minimum of noise and movement. How many times have thorny briar stems and other cover grabbed your jacket sleeve, requiring numerous hand movements to pull them away, often with an accompanying grating noise? And how many times have you been forced to contort yourself into weird positions to maneuver under, around, or through vines or other cover blocking your progress, again often at the expense of unnecessary noise and movements? The solution to this eternal stillhunting problem is to purchase a small set of pruning shears of the type home gardeners use to trim shrubs and ornamental trees. A small cord can be attached to the handle, with the other end tied to your belt, so that you don't have to reach into a pocket to retrieve them. Then, when a thorny branch or weed stem blocks your progress, simply snip it off and allow it to fall softly to the ground.

## GETTING CLOSE TO YOUR BUCK

When a stillhunter spots a buck he often makes the mistake of moving toward the deer. But the first thing he should do is absolutely nothing!

Spend a few moments simply observing the animal. Of utmost importance, study the deer's immediate surroundings for signs of other animals. Whitetails are gregarious creatures. If you rivet your attention on one animal, another deer may see you—and both will bolt.

There have been times when I've patiently stalked a buck for more than an hour by staying at a comfortable distance and slowly moving parallel to his line of travel until adequate cover allowed me to close the distance another few yards or so.

So don't feel you have to hurry. Pretend you're a tomcat stalking a robin in the backyard. You have time to make your moves when the animal is looking in another direction.

By the same token, as you are maintaining a fix on a specific animal, simultaneously study

Moving silently through thick cover can be difficult. One trick is to use a
pair of pruning shears to snip occasional brambles that lie in your path.

the terrain ahead of his line of travel. You'll want to be on the alert for still other deer that may be farther up ahead, and you'll want to plot your final approach to within shooting range with great care.

A couple of times I have actually had to move slowly at a quartering-away angle from a deer, increasing the distance between us. This was necessary in order to stay in the shadows rather than step into a brightly illuminated opening, or to use certain cover or terrain configurations to my advantage.

Despite all of these strategies, every still-hunter will occasionally be detected and the deer will bound away, white banner waving astern. It's simply part of the game. But don't be discouraged; you may still have a chance at that particular animal.

Unlike mule deer and elk, which may travel many miles when they are spooked, whitetails are homebodies that do not like to venture out of their familiar territories. One scientific study of deer equipped with radio collars revealed that the average flight distance of an alarmed buck is only 165 yards. Then the animal dives back into cover and resumes skulking along, and within ten minutes often forgets what it was that routed it out in the first place.

So my advice is this: When you flush a deer and he runs away, sit down and wait a full fifteen minutes. Then, after determining the general direction in which the deer departed, begin stillhunting again, but never follow the animal directly because both alarmed and unalarmed whitetails continually monitor their backtrails. Instead, travel in a wide arc to the right or left, and regain contact at another point.

One time, much to my chagrin, I was stalking a deer when it simply bedded down facing in my direction. With all of his senses now on alert, I knew it would be a futile endeavor to try to move even one step closer. So I simply leaned against a tree trunk, became an inanimate part of the forest, and waited. A full hour later—and I was very tired and cramped—the deer finally rose to his feet and continued ambling along. As it happened, I didn't get that deer, yet I know I couldn't have put forth a better effort.

Then there are the times when you can tell which direction a deer is moving, circle widely to get ahead of him, and then play the waiting game. If you're lucky, you may have to move only a few hundred yards, stop behind a convenient shrub or tree trunk, and let *him* close the distance to you.

# 18

# Advanced Drive Strategies

One of the great shortcomings in the way people perceive things is that too often they equate bigger with better, and the way many deer hunters evaluate prospective hunting grounds is a splendid example. Every year, legions of hunters flood into huge forested areas, thinking there will be more deer there, and bigger bucks, and that if enough hunters are assembled to drive the animals the results should be impressive. They don't consider that a mere ten-acre briar patch behind a rural farmhouse may be the secret hiding place of the biggest buck in the county. But I know better, because I own one of those very farmhouses, and one of the lessons we've repeatedly learned over the years is that a piece of cover that is big enough to hide a rabbit is big enough to hide a deer. Consequently, I'm a strong proponent of short drives in which the cover hunted is generally no larger than about twenty acres (although the farm itself, or tract of public land, may be much larger).

Huge, unbroken tracts of land take an eternity to drive. Even if numerous hunters participate, they simply cannot properly push all the cover or guard all the possible exits, and this allows the deer far too many escape options. When you're driving smaller tracts of heavy cover, however, efficiency soars because the drivers are less likely to wander astray and allow deer to slip back between them. Also, stand hunters can quickly get into their proper positions. It's also less time-consuming to remove deer from the field so the next drive can begin without undue delay.

Finally, small tracts of land are generally overlooked by the masses of other hunters heading for the sprawling forestlands, so you won't have much competition. You may even find more deer, because they've retreated into such tiny, undisturbed hideouts as hunting pressure mounts elsewhere.

In these times of increasingly posted lands, a small group of courteous hunters stands a better chance of gaining access to private property than a caravan of vehicles pulling into a farmer's driveway.

I once participated in a drive in which ten hunters were placed on stand and twenty-five drivers attempted to move deer in their direction through a two-mile-long tract of brambles

When hunting pressure mounts on large, unbroken tracts of land, deer commonly sneak into small, unnoticed segments of cover to escape. Short drives, in cover no larger than twenty acres, can produce whopper bucks.

and brush. It was massive confusion, not to mention the fact that it took over an hour to drop off each hunter at his designated position and another hour to actually make the push. I wasn't surprised when only a single doe was taken. That's why most of my drives these days employ less than eight hunters.

Exactly how many hunters should be standers, and how many drivers, depends upon the nature of the terrain. If it's relatively open cover, where visibility is wide-ranging and drivers can space themselves a good distance apart with little worry of deer slipping back between them, only two drivers may be sufficient. However, if it's junglelike cover where visibility is restricted to a few yards, it's better to have as many drivers as possible working in close-ranked formation with stand hunters posted at the most crucial escape routes. You've

heard the old adage "too many cooks spoil the broth." The same thing applies to a hunting party in which everyone voices differing opinions as to how the drive should be executed. When this happens, too much debate and confusion often cripple what should otherwise be an effective effort.

Much wiser is for the group to nominate one person to be the drivemaster. He may not necessarily be the hunter who has taken the most bucks over the years but the one who is the most familiar with the terrain to be hunted.

Quite often, when we are planning to stage drives on a farm or private tract of land, we invite the landowner or perhaps his teenage sons to join the hunt. After all, they live there year-round, they see deer almost every day, they know every square yard of their property, and they know the travel routes deer take when alarmed. These individuals can be helpful in deciding where to post stand hunters and how drivers should approach certain segments of cover.

## FINDING THE ESCAPE HATCHES

No drive is worth a hoot if deer spurt out and standers have not been properly placed to intercept them. Prior to the drive, hunters should get together and study aerial photos and topo maps and ask themselves, "Where are the escape routes deer are most likely to use?"

This is relatively easy if you simply keep in mind that deer seldom run cross-country across open ground but prefer to use a travel corridor through heavy cover to slip out of one area and into another.

Examples of the types of cover and terrain we like to drive include: narrow gullies or ravines which are choked with downed timber but are no more than 200 yards in length; rectangular-shaped pine plantations of no more than 5 acres, with immature trees having dense whorls of branches close to the ground; rectangular-shaped standing cornfields no larger than 5 acres; willow bars along watercourses no wider than 50 yards and no longer than 200 yards; narrow hollows with almost impenetrable stands of honeysuckle, laurel or rhododendron; briar patches or multiflora rose jungles no larger than 10 acres; tag alder thickets bordering stream bottoms; swampy lowlands no larger than 10 acres with pole timber, blowdowns, at least several inches of standing water and occasional dry hummocks; former fields and croplands now lying fallow which have grown up in

Standing cornfields can offer excellent drive opportunities. Find the escape hatches where deer will predictably exit the corn to gain access to other, distant cover.

Most hunters will avoid swamps if they contain standing water, and mature bucks sense this. These are good places for deer drives.

If there is a big buck in cover where a drive is staged, he'll be the first deer out of there, or he won't come out at all.

ADVANCED DRIVE STRATEGIES    185

brush and thick regenerative saplings such as sassafras, sumac and crabapple of no more than 10 acres in size; and finally, former burns and clearcuts "coming back" into successive vegetation and young trees.

When a mature buck is hiding in a relatively small piece of cover and the cover is driven, that big buck will either be the first deer out of there or he won't come out at all. Big bucks are extremely security conscious, and when alarmed will leave an area hastily.

A hunter who is designated to wait on stand must exercise great care in hiking to his waiting station. If a big buck is bedded relatively close by and hears the hunter moving into position, he will know there's danger in that general area and run in another direction if the approaching drivers succeed in routing him out.

So when moving to your stand, take the long, roundabout way if necessary and sneak into position as quietly as possible. Also, once you've selected your vantage point, do not later change your mind and decide that perhaps somewhere else fifty yards to your right or left might be better. Your partners may have already begun the drive, and if a buck decides to leave the area by coming your way, he will be well ahead of any does or younger bucks in the region and may very well detect your movement as you change locations.

If the drivers move one or more bucks through your general area but you are not rewarded with a shot, don't despair. Simply remember the deer's route of travel. Then, when you drive the area again several days or even weeks later, move your stand accordingly, for when the buck is alarmed yet again he'll likely use the very same escape corridor.

By the same token, those hunters who are to act as drivers should allow their stand hunters plenty of time to get into position. It's simply a wasted effort to begin the drive five minutes too early, before the standers are well situated in their intercept locations.

If there is one thing that typifies a classic deer drive, it is the shouting and whistling of the drivers. We've learned, however, that "silent" drives are often far more effective. We stage our drives during both the bowhunting and gun seasons. When we're bowhunting, we don't want to risk wounding deer that are wildly jackrabbiting through the cover. Also, bucks are less likely to pinpoint the locations of silent drivers. Whenever a buck does peg the whereabouts of a driver and attempts to skirt him, the deer often blunders right into the path of another driver he didn't know was there. We've learned that silent drivers are often awarded just as many shooting opportunities as their partners stationed on stands in the distance.

In tying all of this together, it should be clear that if a combination of does and small bucks passes a stand hunter's location, the drive party can be certain any larger bucks in the immediate vicinity have decided to hold tight; otherwise, they would have been the first ones out.

Actually, this is far more common than most hunters realize. Big bucks select their hiding places with craft and cunning, and they are reluctant to abandon them. They know that rising from their beds and exposing themselves greatly increases their vulnerability. Consequently, when a hunter treads through their area, deer often lower their chins to the ground and don't even blink.

After a drive is over, if members of your group believe there still is a buck in the cover, there's only one thing to do. Drive the same cover a second time, or even a third, until the buck is either routed out or everyone is convinced he wasn't there in the first place.

Don't make the mistake of driving the cover in the same manner as before. Try something different, such as driving the cover in the opposite direction with your stand hunters placed in the vicinity of where the drivers began on the previous drive. On succeeding days, drive the cover from still other directions. This way the deer will be confused and not know from which direction to expect danger. Nor will they ever know the surest escape route to avoid being detected by the hunters placed on stand.

## THE ONE-MAN DRIVE

A solo drive is just the ticket when all members of the hunting party prefer to wait on conventional stands overlooking deer trails, but one hunter has already taken his buck and wants to help his partners fill their tags by "playing dog."

Standers climb into their perches or ground blinds in pre-dawn darkness for the customary morning watch. But then about 10 a.m. the lone driver begins hiking randomly through the cover without regard to wind direction. He doesn't make a lot of noise, but he isn't entirely silent. I often whistle softly to myself as though I'm on a routine hike or a forestry worker doing a timber survey.

Since deer commonly see such people afield, a lone individual who is not making an attempt to be too "sneaky" doesn't usually alarm them too much. They simply get up and move, using one of their established trails to relocate in an adjacent area. One driver can keep deer slowly circulating all day, and eventually his partners should have shooting opportunities.

## THE TWO-MAN DRIVE

The two-man drive is perfect for a couple of hunting pals. One of the best strategies was developed by my pal Bob Sheppard of Carrolton, Alabama.

A hunter who has already taken his buck can instruct his partners where to wait on stand while he hikes through cover to keep deer circulating.

"Radio-tracking studies have demonstrated that when a deer is spooked out of a specific area by a human, the deer will invariably travel only a short distance straightaway, whereupon it turns right or left for 150 to 200 yards and then reverses its line of travel," Bob explained.

The dynamite technique Sheppard and his partner use works anywhere in the country; it can be used by gun hunters or bowhunters; and the actual size of the cover doesn't make any difference as long as it is at least 400 yards in length.

"My partner and I space ourselves about 150 to 200 yards apart so that we are barely out of sight of each other, and then we begin slowly stillhunting parallel to each other through the length of the cover," Sheppard continued. "We keep in close contact with each other by alternately blowing on crow calls."

The call enables the hunters to remain parallel to each other, so one doesn't fall too far behind or get too far ahead of his partner. If one hunter jumps a deer and sees its white flag moving out ahead of him but does not have a clear shot, he immediately gives five short blasts on the call. At this signal, his partner comes to a halt and drops to a kneeling position for five minutes.

"We know that when a deer turns, it may go either right or left before turning again and reversing its line of travel, so there is a fifty-fifty chance the kneeling partner will very shortly see the deer coming toward him," said Sheppard. "If the kneeling partner does not see a deer coming his way during the allotted five-minute time frame, it

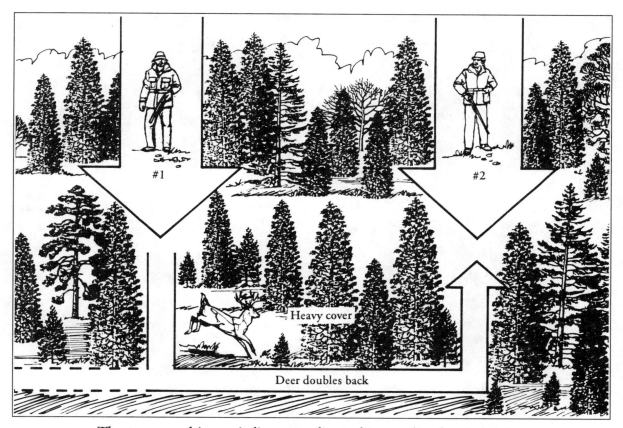

**The two-man drive capitalizes on radio-tracking studies that reveal that driven deer travel straightaway, then turn and reverse their direction.**

can be presumed the deer turned the opposite way. At this time, the kneeling hunter now gives two short and two long blasts on his crow call, which is the signal to resume stillhunting. One very long blast on the call is the signal to regroup and talk or recover a deer that was shot."

## THE LINE DRIVE

Let's say there are very few small tracts of deer habitat in the particular area you hunt. You live in a region where huge, unbroken tracts of national forest or state forest land predominate, much of which is hundreds of square acres in size or even larger.

Now is when the very essence of moving deer takes on critical meaning, because it would take dozens of drivers and dozens more hunters on stand to stage an effective maneuver. In this situation, we like to use a line-drive, which does not entail the use of stand hunters and thus saves time moving people around.

Refer to your aerial photo and carefully study the terrain, looking for open ground bordering one side of the huge forestland. It might be in the form of pasture, meadowland, prairieland or low-growing cropland such as wheat or oats.

Next, line up as many hunters as are present (six or seven is perfect) and space each of them a comfortable distance apart so that each can just barely see an occasional flash of orange from his partners on either side. Each hunter then slowly begins stillhunting through the cover, keeping the line straight.

**In participating in a line drive, you're not likely to see a deer you jumped. Instead, you'll see a buck passing in front of you put up by your partner on your right or left.**

When a buck rises from his bed, he is usually reluctant to run straight away from the advancing drivers. Possibly he knows that eventually he'll emerge from cover into the open. Instead, he'll often run just a short distance ahead of the line and then turn right or left, traveling across the face of the drive in order to stay in the woods and providing an easy broadside target.

## WHEN DEER DOUBLE BACK

Another friend, Bob Becker, of St. Louis, is equally inventive when it comes to engineering devious drives.

One ruse of woods-wise bucks, especially where the cover is so thick it would choke a gopher, is to hunker down tight in their beds when drivers approach. After the drivers have passed, the deer then rise to their feet and begin slipping back in the opposite direction, leaving the drive party to conclude no animals were in that particular area.

To counter this move, Bob employs a "fish-hook drive." Two hunters are placed on stand, while five others spread out as drivers. Then the drive-line begins pushing through the cover. However, two of the hunters on the drive-line have instructions to go only about

Long, narrow strips of cover are ideal for drives because a deer's escape options are limited, often causing it to double back.

two-thirds of the way through the cover. Then they are supposed to about-face and begin stillhunting in the direction from which they've just come. Frequently, these are the two hunters that see all the action because they spot bucks the drive-line previously walked right by and which are now attempting to slip out the back door.

Now, here's the intriguing thing about all of this. Any buck which has doubled back to get behind the drivers may indeed ascertain what the drivers are up to when they engage in their fishhook maneuver. At this, the deer can then be counted upon to double back yet a second time, to get behind the drivers once again. And this will take them to the stand hunters.

I like drives, and especially ones of this type, because they're not only loads of fun but tax the ingenuity of all participants. Very often, they also add a hefty sag to the camp meatpole.